P9-CFJ-281

Western Democracy at Risk

Other Books of Related Interest

Opposing Viewpoints Series

American Values
America's Global Influence
Democracy
Dictatorships
Election Spending

At Issue Series

Are America's Wealthy Too Powerful?
Does the US Two-Party System Still Work?
Does the World Hate the US?
The United Nations

Current Controversies Series

Federal Elections
Patriotism
Politics and Media
US Government Corruption

> "Congress shall make no law … abridging the freedom of speech, or of the press."
>
> *First Amendment to the US Constitution*

The basic foundation of our democracy is the First Amendment guarantee of freedom of expression. The Opposing Viewpoints series is dedicated to the concept of this basic freedom and the idea that it is more important to practice it than to enshrine it.

Western Democracy at Risk

Avery Elizabeth Hurt, Book Editor

Published in 2018 by Greenhaven Publishing, LLC
353 3rd Avenue, Suite 255, New York, NY 10010

First Edition

Articles in Greenhaven Publishing anthologies are often edited for length to meet page requirements. In addition, original titles of these works are changed to clearly present the main thesis and to explicitly indicate the author's opinion. Every effort is made to ensure that Greenhaven Publishing accurately reflects the original intent of the authors. Every effort has been made to trace the owners of the copyrighted material.

Cover image: Elijah Nouvelage/Getty Images

Library of Congress Cataloging-in-Publication Data

Names: Hurt, Avery Elizabeth, editor.
Title: Western democracy at risk / Avery Elizabeth Hurt, book editor.
Description: First edition. | New York : Greenhaven Publishing, [2018] |
Series: Opposing viewpoints | Audience: Grade 9 to 12. |
Includes bibliographical references and index.
Identifiers: LCCN 2017033246| ISBN 9781534501737
(library bound) | ISBN 9781534501799 (pbk.)
Subjects: LCSH: Democracy—Western countries—Juvenile literature. |
Western countries—Politics and government—Juvenile literature.
Classification: LCC JC423 .W387 2018 | DDC 320.9182/1--dc23
LC record available at https://lccn.loc.gov/2017033246

Manufactured in the United States of America

Website: http://greenhavenpublishing.com

Contents

Chapter 3: Does the US System of Representation Preclude a True Democracy?

Chapter 4: What Does the Future Hold for Western Democracy?

The Importance of Opposing Viewpoints

Perhaps every generation experiences a period in time in which the populace seems especially polarized, starkly divided on the important issues of the day and gravitating toward the far ends of the political spectrum and away from a consensus-facilitating middle ground. The world that today's students are growing up in and that they will soon enter into as active and engaged citizens is deeply fragmented in just this way. Issues relating to terrorism, immigration, women's rights, minority rights, race relations, health care, taxation, wealth and poverty, the environment, policing, military intervention, the proper role of government—in some ways, perennial issues that are freshly and uniquely urgent and vital with each new generation—are currently roiling the world.

If we are to foster a knowledgeable, responsible, active, and engaged citizenry among today's youth, we must provide them with the intellectual, interpretive, and critical-thinking tools and experience necessary to make sense of the world around them and of the all-important debates and arguments that inform it. After all, the outcome of these debates will in large measure determine the future course, prospects, and outcomes of the world and its peoples, particularly its youth. If they are to become successful members of society and productive and informed citizens, students need to learn how to evaluate the strengths and weaknesses of someone else's arguments, how to sift fact from opinion and fallacy, and how to test the relative merits and validity of their own opinions against the known facts and the best possible available information. The landmark series Opposing Viewpoints has been providing students with just such critical-thinking skills and exposure to the debates surrounding society's most urgent contemporary issues for many years, and it continues to serve this essential role with undiminished commitment, care, and rigor.

The key to the series's success in achieving its goal of sharpening students' critical-thinking and analytic skills resides in its title—

Opposing Viewpoints. In every intriguing, compelling, and engaging volume of this series, readers are presented with the widest possible spectrum of distinct viewpoints, expert opinions, and informed argumentation and commentary, supplied by some of today's leading academics, thinkers, analysts, politicians, policy makers, economists, activists, change agents, and advocates. Every opinion and argument anthologized here is presented objectively and accorded respect. There is no editorializing in any introductory text or in the arrangement and order of the pieces. No piece is included as a "straw man," an easy ideological target for cheap point-scoring. As wide and inclusive a range of viewpoints as possible is offered, with no privileging of one particular political ideology or cultural perspective over another. It is left to each individual reader to evaluate the relative merits of each argument—as he or she sees it, and with the use of ever-growing critical-thinking skills—and grapple with his or her own assumptions, beliefs, and perspectives to determine how convincing or successful any given argument is and how the reader's own stance on the issue may be modified or altered in response to it.

This process is facilitated and supported by volume, chapter, and selection introductions that provide readers with the essential context they need to begin engaging with the spotlighted issues, with the debates surrounding them, and with their own perhaps shifting or nascent opinions on them. In addition, guided reading and discussion questions encourage readers to determine the authors' point of view and purpose, interrogate and analyze the various arguments and their rhetoric and structure, evaluate the arguments' strengths and weaknesses, test their claims against available facts and evidence, judge the validity of the reasoning, and bring into clearer, sharper focus the reader's own beliefs and conclusions and how they may differ from or align with those in the collection or those of their classmates.

Research has shown that reading comprehension skills improve dramatically when students are provided with compelling, intriguing, and relevant "discussable" texts. The subject matter of these collections could not be more compelling, intriguing, or urgently relevant to today's students and the world they are poised to inherit. The anthologized articles and the reading and discussion questions that are included with them also provide the basis for stimulating, lively, and passionate classroom debates. Students who are compelled to anticipate objections to their own argument and identify the flaws in those of an opponent read more carefully, think more critically, and steep themselves in relevant context, facts, and information more thoroughly. In short, using discussable text of the kind provided by every single volume in the Opposing Viewpoints series encourages close reading, facilitates reading comprehension, fosters research, strengthens critical thinking, and greatly enlivens and energizes classroom discussion and participation. The entire learning process is deepened, extended, and strengthened.

For all of these reasons, Opposing Viewpoints continues to be exactly the right resource at exactly the right time—when we most need to provide readers with the critical-thinking tools and skills that will not only serve them well in school but also in their careers and their daily lives as decision-making family members, community members, and citizens. This series encourages respectful engagement with and analysis of opposing viewpoints and fosters a resulting increase in the strength and rigor of one's own opinions and stances. As such, it helps make readers "future ready," and that readiness will pay rich dividends for the readers themselves, for the citizenry, for our society, and for the world at large.

Introduction

> *"Democracy has always had its critics, but now old doubts are being treated with renewed respect as the weaknesses of democracy in its Western strongholds, and the fragility of its influence elsewhere, have become increasingly apparent."*
>
> --*The Economist,* *"What's Gone Wrong with Democracy?"*

According to an account written by James McHenry, one of the delegates to the Constitutional Convention in Philadelphia in 1787, when Benjamin Franklin stepped out of the hall moments after the new constitution had been signed, he was met by a crowd of citizens. One woman asked the great statesman, "Well, what have we got, a monarchy or a republic?" Franklin replied, "A republic, if you can keep it."

Political scientists have long believed in something they call "democratic consolidation," the idea that once a society has developed a democracy and established the norms and institutions that go along with it, those democracies—lacking an exceptionally severe economic or environmental crisis—are very unlikely to slither back into an authoritarian form of government. Democracy in the West seemed like a done deal.

However, recent trends have made scholars question this assumption. According to research by Roberto Stefan Foa and Yascha Mounk, Western democracy is now at risk of "deconsolidation," a process that could, with alarming speed, lead to the end of Western Democracy as we know it.

After gathering data on democracies that have failed or are failing (such as Venezuela) Foa and Mounk identify "warning signs" that indicate a democracy is at risk. Several of these are on the rise in the West. For example, an increasing number of people surveyed say that they do not feel it is necessary to live in a democratic society. An alarming number also approve of having "a strong leader who does not have to bother with parliament or elections."

You don't have to conduct surveys to see signs that democracy is in trouble in the West. In the 2016 presidential election, only 55.7 percent of voting age Americans bothered to vote. Voter turnout is considerably higher in other Western democracies, but even there it has been slipping in recent years. (Voter turnout may be trending back upward in some nations. After decades of decline, turnout for the 2015 Canadian Federal election was the highest it had been since 1993.)

When people do vote, increasing numbers of voters back leaders or parties that threaten democracy. Authoritarian parties, such as the National Front in France and the Dutch Party for Freedom, have garnered a new level of support in recent decades. Though US president Donald Trump didn't win the popular vote (he was elected by an electoral college victory), he did win a surprising amount of support and has since shown an astonishing tendency to ignore or even disparage the norms of democracy and push policies that subvert democratic processes. No matter who is elected, the increasing polarity and divisiveness in many Western governments can make it difficult to govern. The US Congress is the best example of this, but the 2017 election in Britain also highlighted the difficulties of forming a government when the population is so divided.

Not all the damage to Western democracies comes from within. There is credible evidence that Russia attempted to interfere in the 2016 US elections, as well as the 2017 election in France, and it is likely that more interference is yet to be attempted. The effect of Russian efforts to undermine Western democracy remains to be seen, but could be one of the greatest dangers facing the West since the Cold War.

Franklin was right. Keeping that republic may not be easy.

The viewpoints in *Opposing Viewpoints: Western Democracy at Risk* asks relevant questions, in chapters titled "Are the Demands of Modern Democracy Too Much for the Modern World?" "Can Western Democracies Withstand the Recent Trend Toward Authoritarianism?" "Does the US System of Representation Preclude a True Democracy?" and "What Does the Future Hold for Western Democracy?" In the viewpoints that follow, you will read about many of stresses to Western democracy, from people on both sides of the political spectrum and those with no particular ideology other than a belief in the value of democracy. The facts are disturbing, but there is also evidence that the mood in Europe, at least, is moderating. In the closing paragraph of the paper cited above, Mounk and Foa write,

> But neither fate nor destiny decrees that democracy will falter. For now, the window for political agency remains open. Whether democratic deconsolidation will one day be seen as the beginning of the end for liberal democracy depends in good part on the ability of democracy's defenders to heed the warning and to mount a coherent response.

CHAPTER 1

Is Democracy Too Demanding for Today's Citizens?

Chapter Preface

The poet and playwright Oscar Wilde is said to have observed that "socialism would take too many evenings." In his essay "The Soul of Man Under Socialism," Wilde made a fascinating argument for a kind of libertarian socialism he believed would finally address the problems of inequality in modern capitalist society. But this oft-quoted observation about the effort required for such a society applies equally well to democracy in general, whether socialist or capitalist. Being an informed and engaged citizen requires not only scanning your news feed every now and then and voting every two (or perhaps four) years but also a willingness to understand and keep up with the workings of government both local and national, and to take part in that government as a citizen.

In today's world engaged citizens must keep up with policy on a vast array of increasingly complex issues, from health care to taxes to foreign policy. It can sometimes seem as if being a good citizen requires being a polymath (a person with deep knowledge about a lot of different subjects). That is not the only challenge citizens of modern democracies encounter. Finding the time to register to vote, get to polling places at the right times, and having the proper ID when you get there make the basic, entry-level participation of voting difficult for many. And when their governments operate secretly behind closed doors, willfully ignore the will of the people, or neglect or infringe upon the rights of minorities, then citizens are called upon to do much more than just learn and vote. They have to speak up, speak out, and yes, sometimes attend meetings in the evenings.

In this chapter, you will read viewpoints that examine just how educated and informed one has to be to be a citizen in a modern democracy; why so few Americans bother to vote; and just what it means when the people who are taking part in a democracy aren't really people after all.

Viewpoint 1

> *"Big money in politics distorts representation and responsiveness."*

Citizens United Has Damaged US Democracy

Liz Kennedy

In the following viewpoint, Liz Kennedy explains how the Supreme Court decision known as Citizens United *affects the power balance in US democracy. By allowing corporations to support political candidates in the same way individuals do, the court has granted "big money" a disproportionate share of the say in who is elected to public office. Kennedy lists five ways the decision is harmful to democracy, and closes with five ways ordinary citizens are working to repair democracy in the wake of this decision. The viewpoint's numerous notes can be found online. Kennedy is director of government and democratic reform at the Center for American Progress.*

As you read, consider the following questions:

1. What does Kennedy mean by an elite "donor class," and why is this bad for democracy?
2. Why are Congressional candidates influenced by wealthy donors?
3. What is "dark money," and why, according to Kennedy, is this particularly dangerous?

"Top 5 Ways Citizens United Harms Democracy & Top 5 Ways We're Fighting to Take Democracy Back," by Liz Kennedy, Demos, January 15, 2015. Reprinted by permission.

In the five years since the Supreme Court's *Citizens United* decision the dominance of big money over politics and policy has grown, seemingly without restraint and with dire consequences for representative self-government. A functioning democracy requires a government responsive to people considered as political equals, where we each have a say in the public policy decisions that affect our lives. It is profoundly anti-democratic for anyone to be able to purchase political power, and when a small elite makes up a donor class that is able to shape our government and our public policy.

It's not just the amount of money being spent on campaigns and to lobby our elected representatives—which is on the rise and increasingly secret.[1] The problem is that our current system for funding elections allows a few people and special interests to have much more power over the direction of our country than the vast majority of Americans, who have different views on public policy than the wealthy elite.[2] We've been fighting to control the improper influence of money in government, whether from wealthy individuals or corporate interests, since the founding of our republic.[3] But we are at a low point, where large financial interests wield tremendous political power, and much of the blame rests squarely on the Supreme Court and its campaign finance decisions.

Americans across the political spectrum understand that our current rules for using money in politics give the wealthy greater political power and prevent us from having an equal chance to influence the political process,[4] and that government is not serving our interests but rather serving special interests.[5] Comprehensive, structural changes are needed to stop the anti-democratic results of our current system, and many practical solutions already exist to help build a new system.[6] The Supreme Court must reverse course and allow us to adopt common sense rules to reclaim our democratic self-government of, by, and for the people.

Here are five ways *Citizens United* harms democracy and five ways people are fighting back.

Top 5 Ways Citizens United Harms Democracy

1. Big money in politics allows a wealthy elite few to overpower other voices to an unprecedented degree, at all levels of government.

Citizens United declared that it was unconstitutional to restrict a corporation from spending its treasury money to support or attack candidates in elections,[7] and led to unlimited contributions to outside groups such as Super PACs and tax-exempt non-profits.[8] These decisions have allowed concentrated big money in politics to increase,[9] further marginalizing those without vast wealth in our political system.[10] Consider these facts:

- In the 2012 election just 31,385 donors who make up .01 percent of all Americans contributed more than 28 percent of the money spent.[11]
- Small donors do not play a significant role in most political fundraising; campaign money generally comes in donations of $1,000 or more from less than 1 percent of donors.[12] In 2014, in the most competitive races candidates got 86 percent of individual contributions from donors giving more than $200.[13]
- The $313 million raised by President Obama and Mitt Romney from all of their small donors combined—over 4 million people giving less than $200—was matched by just the top 32 donors to Super PACs who gave an average of $9.9 million each.[14] In the 2014 election, just 100 individuals and their spouses contributed 37 percent of the money raised by Super PACS.[15]

These elite few donors become gatekeepers. Since candidates for the House and Senate who spend the most money win the vast majority of the time, our current system leaves our representatives dependent on a tiny slice of the wealthiest few in what is essentially a wealth primary.[16] For example, Sheldon Adelson was the largest individual spender in the 2012 election, famously spending approximately $150 million dollars to advance his political views, $98 million through disclosed channels and the rest through dark money channels like Karl Rove's Crossroads GPS and groups with links to the Kochs.[17] Former White House press secretary under President George W. Bush Ari Fleischer has remarked "certainly the 'Sheldon Primary' is an important primary for any Republican running for president."[18] Tom Steyer, the single largest donor of disclosed political spending in the 2014 elections, has the ability to play the same role in the Democratic Party.[19] Regardless of partisan affiliation, when wealthy individuals and corporate interests can determine who runs, who wins, the agenda, and ultimately the law,[20] our politics risks becoming just a disagreement between rich people.[21]

The dominance of big money in politics has a real impact on elections at all levels, not just federal elections, and is skewing policy at those levels as well. There has been a vast increase in spending in state and local legislative and executive races: $2.2 billion was spent in state elections in the 2014 cycle.[22] For example, in Missouri, multimillionaire Rex Sinquefield is using his wealth to dominate state politics and shape policy to his liking, which includes cutting funding for education.[23] In North Carolina, Art Pope dominated spending behind the Republican takeover of state government in 2012; the Governor then named him budget director and the state cut millions of dollars in social programs and attacked the freedom to vote.[24] Big money politics is also on the rise in judicial races, raising serious questions about impartial justice when judges are raising money from wealthy interests and attorneys who appear before them.[25] Former Justice Sandra Day O'Connor has called attention to the threat of rising spending and politicization of judicial election, saying "if Americans start thinking of judges as politicians in robes, our democracy is in trouble."[26]

The role of money in politics also undermines racial equity. People of color are not adequately represented by elected officials because of the inequities in our money in politics system.[27] At the county, state, and federal level, whites make up 90 percent of our elected leaders, though 37 percent of the U.S. population is people of color; additionally, men make up 71 percent of elected officials, though the electorate is 51 women.[28] As Demos President Heather McGhee writes, "underrepresented in government and among the wealthy interests with the most access to government, African Americans, Latinos, Asian Americans and Native Americans are less able to win policies that would improve their communities, on issues from fair lending to criminal justice."[29] Our unprincipled and unrestrained big money in politics system is a principal barrier preventing the best and the brightest from leading a democracy truly reflective of our diversity.

Citizens United greatly increased the power of corporations over the power of regular Americans. The U.S. Chamber of Commerce was the largest outside dark money spender in the 2014 elections.[30] Judge Nelson of the Montana Supreme Court—whose state's nearly century old Anti-Corruption Act was declared unconstitutional by the Supreme Court as a result of the *Citizens United* decision—aptly described the harm to our democracy:

> it is utter nonsense to think that ordinary citizens or candidates can spend enough to place their experience, wisdom, and views before the voters and keep pace with the virtually unlimited spending capability of corporations to place corporate views before the electorate. In spending ability, bigger really is better; and with campaign advertising and attack ads, quantity counts. In the end, candidates and the public will become mere bystanders in elections.

2. Secret political spending exploded after Citizens United because the disclosure requirements relied on by the Court do not yet exist.

"Dark money"—political spending whose actual source is undisclosed—robs voters of information they need to make educated decisions and to exercise accountability. In *Citizens United*, the Court affirmed the constitutionality of disclosure requirements by an 8-1 majority. Justice Kennedy believed transparency would enable voters "to make informed decisions and give proper weight to different speakers and messages." But there isn't an effective system to require disclosure at the federal level, or in many states. As a result of the lack of an effective disclosure regime, a new ability and willingness to spend unlimited undisclosed sums, and a failure of government, in most cases, to take corrective action, secret political spending has shot up to historic highs.

In 2014, dubbed the "dark money" election, media spending topped $1 billion and about 40 percent of ads were purchased by dark money groups.[31] In the most competitive Senate races, more than 70 percent of the outside spending benefitting the ten winning candidates was dark money.[32] Dark money has risen exponentially in the cycles since *Citizens United*: organizations that don't disclose their donors spent over $300 million to affect the 2012 election, more than twice as much as in the 2010 elections on the heels of the decision.

Federal disclosure requirements do not currently reach much of the new political spending, which is directed through channels outside of the traditional political players such as parties, candidate campaign committees, and traditional political action committees. Tax-exempt nonprofit forms like 501(c)(4) social welfare groups and 501(c)(6) trade associations are being used as turbo-charged political organizations that accept and spend unlimited sums in elections to support or attack candidates without telling the public where the money comes from.[33] The underlying donors to these groups remain hidden behind technicalities.

When political spenders can hide behind meaningless—or worse, misleading—names, it robs voters of information they need to assess political messages. Corporate donors can prevent "citizens and shareholders [from reacting] to the speech of corporate entities in a proper way" by cloaking their political spending through conduit organizations that disguise their true identity and agendas. For example, the "Coalition-Americans Working for Real Change" was a business organization opposed to organized labor, and "Citizens for Better Medicare" was funded by the pharmaceutical industry.[34] Dark money groups are now soliciting contributions on the promise of donor anonymity: the Wisconsin governor's campaign urged deep-pocketed donors to give to the Wisconsin Club for Growth because it "can accept Corporate and Personal donations without limitations and no donors disclosure."[35] Stephen Colbert compared these practices to money laundering.[36]

3. The purported "independence" of outside spending is often a farce, allowing for evasion of contribution limits and disclosure requirements.

Since *Buckley v. Valeo* the Supreme Court has supported treating "coordinated" spending by outside groups as contributions, because "the ultimate effect is the same as if the [spender] had contributed the dollar amount . . . to the candidate." And the *Citizens United* decision hangs on the majority's assertion that outside spending can't pose a corruption risk because it is purportedly "independent" of any candidate.[37] But the frequent lack of actual "independence" for outside spending means this spending ought to be considered coordinated and regulated as a contribution, and it undercuts the Court's theory that the government doesn't have a sufficient interest in adopting common sense rules to limit these unlimited spending channels.

While rules exist to regulate coordination between candidates and outside groups,[38] Federal Elections Commission Commissioner Ann Ravel allows that they are "sadly murky."[39] Sophisticated political players have evaded them in all but their most technical sense, and they've gone unenforced by a broken FEC.[40] "The New Soft Money" report by Professor Daniel Tokaji and Renata Strause quotes an anonymous campaign operative, saying "at the end of the day, it's all just kind of a fiction—it's just kind of a farce, the whole campaign finance non-coordination thing."[41]

Professor Tokaji notes that new practices "may bend common sense, but not necessarily the law" since "a lot of things you and I would consider coordination are not coordination under the law."[42] For example, we've seen the rise of single candidate Super

PACs that are founded and run by former campaign associates, funded by family and friends, and for whom the candidate is allowed to solicit funds from donors.[43] In the 2014 elections, Twitter was used to communicate strategic information between a Republican campaign committee and two outside groups—the groups may have run afoul of campaign laws because the information in the tweets could be considered a donation.[44] Senator Mitch McConnell released b-roll footage of himself to be used by his supporters;[45] Senator Jeanne Shaheen posted potential ad scripts on her website which may have telegraphed the messages her campaign thought would be most helpful for outside groups to air; and Senator-elect Thom Tillis posted a media strategy memo presenting the campaign's assessment of its need for television and digital ad support.[46]

4. Big money in politics distorts representation and responsiveness, preventing effective policy solutions supported by majorities of Americans.

Citizens United exacerbates the domination of the donor class over public policy outcomes. Research shows that government responds to the public policy preferences of the donor class and not the preferences of the majority of Americans in the middle and working class. [47] When the views of the richest 10 percent differ from the rest of us, the 10 percent trumps the 90 percent.[48]

This research also confirms that the very wealthy have starkly different policy priorities than the general public, especially on economic issues.[49] For example, over two-thirds of the public believes that "the government in Washington ought to see to it that everyone who wants to work can find a job", but among the wealthy only 19 percent agreed with that statement—a disparity of more than 3 to 1.[50] Similarly, 78 percent of the public supports a minimum wage high enough that no family with a full time worker falls below the poverty line while only 40 percent of the wealthy agree, a nearly 2 to 1 disparity.[51] Americans across the political spectrum understand that money in politics is the reason their representatives are more responsive to private interests with financial resources than to the public interest.[52] This distortion of representation and government responsiveness is blocking necessary policy solutions to pressing problems supported by a majority of Americans on economic, environmental, and social issues.

Public servants owe a duty of loyalty to the people they represent, not just to those who fund campaigns. If government decisions can be bought by private wealth we end up with "an elite or ruling class of people whose power derives from their wealth"—the definition of plutocracy.[53] The infrastructure for funding our political system should avoid this risk, not intensify it.

5. The Supreme Court's decisions have distorted the Constitution by preventing common-sense rules to protect representative self-government.

The Court's jurisprudence, and current political intransigence, is preventing us from protecting our government from being dominated by big money. The Court has misunderstood the true need for common-sense rules to protect democracy for forty years, since the 1976 post-Watergate case *Buckley v. Valeo* declared that limiting spending in elections was unconstitutional. And now the Roberts Court has struck down each money in politics regulation that has come before it; *McCutcheon v. FEC* was the seventh case to strike down a campaign finance law since 2006.

Citizens United radically narrowed the government's interest in regulating money in politics.[54] The Supreme Court used to recognize that people have a compelling interest in protecting government from "the corrosive and distorting effects of immense aggregations of wealth that are accumulated with the help of the corporate form and that have little or no correlation to the public's support for the corporation's political ideas."[55] Just as an unregulated economic marketplace does not necessarily produce free and fair trade, an unregulated system of money in politics can lead to a system where financial-might-makes-right.

The rights of democratic citizenship must mean that self-determination is not dependent on wealth. Because access and influence gained through money is closed off to all but a few Americans, it is an illegitimate source of democratic political power. There are some things that aren't for sale; in a democracy, the power of government must be one of them.[56]

Top 5 Ways We're Fighting to Take Democracy Back

Millions of Americans are fighting back—building a national democracy movement and demanding real structural changes to the way money is used to exert power and influence in our political system.

1. We must reclaim the Constitution to empower the people to adopt common-sense rules to protect our democratic government from being dominated by big money.

The Supreme Court's money in politics jurisprudence is deeply flawed and fails to reflect our Constitution's core values of equal voice and democratic accountability. In response to careful development of new legal theories and changing public opinion, the Court has reversed itself in the past to correct fundamental mistakes on critical issues such as slavery and racial segregation, New Deal economic regulations, and marriage equality. More and more scholars, jurists, elected officials and advocates understand that a similar change in course is needed now to ensure that we can protect democratic self-government from domination by big money interests.

Citizens United has come under withering critique.[57] Justice Ruth Bader Ginsburg has said "if there is one decision I would overrule, it is *Citizens United*. I think the notion that we have all the democracy that money can buy strays so far from what our democracy is supposed to be."[58] Leading First Amendment scholar and former University of Chicago Law School Dean Geoffrey

Stone writes "that these five justices persist in invalidating these regulations under a perverse and unwarranted interpretation of the First Amendment is, to be blunt, a travesty. These decisions will be come to be counted as among the worst decisions in the history of the Supreme Court."[59] Judge Guido Calabresi of the Second Circuit has written that "all is not well with this law" and predicts that "just as constitutional law eventually came to embrace the concept [of one-person-one-vote], so too will it come to accept the importance of the antidistortion interest in the law of campaign finance."[60]

The public also rejects the Roberts Court's distorted vision of the Constitution regarding money in politics. Fifty-nine percent of the public says money is not a form of free speech, and only 24 percent says it is, which has changed dramatically since before the *Citizens United* decision.[61] If the courts fail to understand the true nature of the problem of money in politics, the people will serve as the ultimate check. Seventy-three percent support a constitutional amendment to overturn Citizens United; this includes a 26-point margin among Republicans and a 56-point advantage among independents.[62] In September 2014, after 16 states and 550 municipalities passed resolutions demanding *Citizens United* be overturned, and at the urging of more than 3.5 million petition signers,[63] a majority of the U.S. Senate voted to support a constitutional amendment to empower people to adopt common-sense rules for using money in politics. Citizens are actually united around a shared support for necessary structural solutions to control the domination of money over our politics.[64]

2. We must support the participation of small donors and empower every voice through public financing.

To counter the influence of big money in politics we need structures that encourage small donors to get involved. Public financing programs that match small donations with public funds increase the impact of small contributions and incentivize candidates to reach out to people in their communities. Candidates will spend more time hearing from regular voters, rather than only from the elite donor class (who may or may not be constituents). The Government by the People Act, introduced by Representative Sarbanes with 160 co-sponsors, provides a multiple match of 6-1 for small donations which amplifies voices of ordinary Americans, creates a tax credit to allow all citizens to support the candidates of their choosing, and has a mechanism to address the threat of outside spending.[65] This public financing bill is supported by 67 percent of voters who heard arguments for and against the program,[66] and 75 percent of voters from groups that make up the Rising American Electorate.[67]

Investing in small donor democracy through public financing is the best policy we can currently enact to democratize the influence of money in politics, and has been very successful in practice. New York City's small donor matching funds have diversified the donor pool and increased the ability of candidates of color to run and win.[68] In Connecticut, 90 percent of legislative candidates and both gubernatorial candidates participated in that state's clean elections program. Once candidates were no longer exclusively dependent on wealthy donors and businesses, the influence of lobbyists decreased, and elected representatives became more responsive to the public will and passed popular programs such as guaranteeing paid sick leave to workers and raising the minimum wage.[69]

Since *Citizens United*, more jurisdictions are working to adopt and strengthen their public financing programs. In Montgomery County, Maryland, one of the largest county governments in the country, the county commission voted unanimously to empower small voters by matching small contributions with public funds.[70] Voters in Maine[71] and North Carolina[72] are organizing to fight back against cuts to their public financing programs. New York State came close to passing a very popular Fair Elections bill in the past two years, modeled on the successful New York City program, and ought to be a leader in the nation.[73]

3. We must adopt effective disclosure requirements for political spending because voters deserve this information and knowledge is necessary for accountability.

Citizens United recognized that "prompt disclosure of expenditures can provide shareholders and citizens with the information needed to hold corporations and elected officials accountable for their positions and supporters."[74] Disclosure of political spending serves voters' interests in knowing who is funding a political message and about a candidate's financial allegiances; protects against corrupt political deal-making; and prevents circumvention of campaign finance protections such as contribution limits by allowing monitoring.

The Federal Election Commission (FEC), the principal agency tasked with enforcing federal campaign finance laws, has unfortunately narrowed the disclosure requirements included in the Bipartisan Campaign Reform Act, but that action was rejected by a federal court.[75] The judge found that the rule created an "easily exploited loophole that allows the true sponsors of advertisements to hide behind dubious and misleading names"[76] and concluded "the fact that some contributors 'just don't want their names known' does not provide grounds to override a clear Congressional choice in favor of transparency."[77]

There is much work that other federal agencies can and must do to prevent abuse and provide transparency so that voters may exercise accountability. The U.S. Securities and Exchange Commission (SEC) has received more than one million public comments, the most in agency history, on a proposed rule to require publicly traded corporations to disclose their political spending.[78] The SEC has the authority and the responsibility to promulgate this rule for the protection of investors and in the public interest in response the newly allowed corporate political spending resulting from *Citizens United*.[79] The Internal Revenue Service (IRS), is addressing the issue of nonprofits abusing their tax-exempt status to spend unlimited money to influence elections without disclosing their donors by engaging in a rulemaking to establish bright lines for political activity by nonprofits. And the Federal Communications Commission (FCC) moved this summer to require all broadcasters to put their political files online, providing significantly improved transparency about ad buys.[80] There is now a petition pending before the FCC to have the Commission enforce existing laws and regulations requiring broadcasters to disclose the "true identity" of the sponsor of a political ad.[81]

President Obama can and should issue an executive order requiring disclosure of political spending by government contractors. Without transparency for political spending by those competing for government contracts, the public cannot detect if those seeking to do business with the government are providing financial support to government officials to increase their chances of receiving public contracts.[82] Pay-to-play is corrupt and corrupting,[83] and this type of crony capitalism has no place in our society.

In the face of newfound congressional intransigence against political transparency, Congress has failed to act to update federal disclosure laws to cover the new spending allowed by the *Citizens United*.[84] But there are important opportunities to improve disclosure requirements at the state and local level particularly in the face of increased spending in state and local races. In response to Citizens United, states have updated and expanded their disclosure regulations and enforcement; California,[85] Delaware,[86] Massachusetts,[87] Maryland,[88] Hawaii,[89] Vermont[90] and North Carolina[91] each passed new disclosure laws.[92]

4. We must prevent the evasion of contribution limits and disclosure requirements by strengthening anti-coordination rules to enforce actual independence for any outside spending.

Anti-coordination rules are necessary to enforce the requirement that unlimited spending be truly "independent" of the candidate. Without effective rules regulating coordination, it is easy for sophisticated political players to circumvent contribution limits, rendering them ineffectual. But there are specific steps that can be taken to address current abuses: for example, coordination rules should reach all forms of outside spending; fundraising by candidates for "independent" groups should be treated as coordination; republication of candidate materials should be considered coordination, and certain shared staff or consultants should be considered indicia of coordination.[93] Non-independent outside spending should be treated as contributions of benefit to the candidate, and therefore subject to contribution limits.[94]

Effective anti-coordination rules also help prevent evasion of donor disclosure because they discourage the formation of dark money vehicles that exist in parallel to candidate and official political action committee channels yet can be just as useful to a candidate. If such rules were enforced, it would be a disincentive for the huge growth in outside spending because it might be somewhat less helpful to the candidate without the level of coordination that is currently allowed. Since the traditional candidate, party, and political action committee channels are subject to disclosure requirements, this could help improve transparency for political spending.

The FEC should strengthen and enforce its anti-coordination rules to play a more effective role in preventing the circumvention of the remaining contribution limits and ensuring that campaign-finance disclosure is robust enough to ensure that citizens have sufficient information to evaluate political messages.[95] State and local jurisdictions can take steps to protect their elections as well; Philadelphia's Board of Ethics recently adopted rules to prevent coordination from vitiating the independence of outside spending by restricting candidate fundraising for outside groups, and categorizing costs for reproducing a candidate's campaign materials as contributions.[96]

5. We must continue to take action to demand solutions to the problem of big money's domination of democratic government.

Public support to solve the problem of money in politics is large and growing across party lines. Ninety-two percent say it is important that "our elected leaders reduce the influence of money in political elections."[97] Sixty-one percent of voters, up from 51 percent in 2011, say we need to make "major changes" to the way campaigns are financed in the U.S.[98] The public supports limits on not just contributions but also political spending, for both candidates and outside groups. Ninety percent say they would support a federal law that imposes tough, new campaign finance laws.[99] Seventy-nine percent support limiting the amount of money U.S. House and Senate candidates can raise and spend on their campaigns.[100] Seventy-six percent say unaffiliated groups should be limited in the amount they can spend on political ads during a campaign.[101]

People are standing up and demanding change.[102] A growing movement of civil rights, economic justice, environmental, consumer groups, students, business, and faith groups are coming together to commit to enacting transformative change by reducing the role of big money and strengthening our democracy. This past spring, in response to the *McCutcheon* decision, people across the country held 150 demonstrations in 41 states to protest against the court's destructive decisions. Now, in advance of the fifth anniversary of *Citizens United*, over a hundred groups—the largest collection of diverse groups ever aligned behind such an extensive set of money in politics policy solutions—have signed on to a Unity Statement of Principles: Solutions to the Undue Influence of Money in Politics.[103]

The courts and our elected representatives must respond.

> *"Equality means first and foremost the equality of rights under a just rule of law, with the basic right of every individual being the right to noninterference."*

Higher Taxes on the Wealthy Would Violate Constitutional Property Rights

James A. Dorn

In the following excerpted viewpoint, James A. Dorn examines a widely read 2014 book Capital in the Twenty-First Century, *by French economist Thomas Piketty. This book demonstrates that since the industrial revolution, the amount of wealth owned by a small group of private interests has eclipsed that held by nations, contributing to a huge increase in global wealth inequality. It goes on to argue that in order to prevent this situation from creating economic or political instability, inequality could and should be countered by increasing taxes on the wealthy. Dorn argues that while Pikkety's proposal would restore some measure of equality, it would also run counter to cherished ideals of freedom and democracy. Dorn is senior fellow at the Cato Institute and editor of the* Cato Journal.

"Equality, Justice, and Freedom: A Constitutional Perspective," by James A. Dorn, Cato Journal, Vol. 34, No. 3 (Fall 2014). Reprinted by Permission.

As you read, consider the following questions:

1. According to Dorn, how has the notion of "equality" been eroded in what he calls the "modern redistributive state"?
2. What sorts of rights was the US Constitution designed to protect, according to the author?
3. How does Dorn define "equality of rights" in this essay?

The publication of Thomas Piketty's best-selling book *Capital in the Twenty-First Century* (2014) has raised awareness of the rising inequality of income and wealth. The author argues that such inequality threatens democratic values and should be reversed by imposing steeply progressive income and wealth taxes on the rich and near-rich. His policies, if implemented, would create more equal outcomes but undermine the principles of freedom and justice that are the essence of the U.S. Constitution.

[...]

The constitutional perspective on equality—namely, equal rights and freedom under a rule of law—has been eroded as the redistributive state has grown. Equality has come to mean equal outcomes and "equal opportunity," in the sense of equal starting positions, rather than equal rights under a just rule of law. The trend toward what Anderson and Hill (1980) have called the "transfer society" has been encouraged by a complacent judiciary that has split the constitutional rights fabric in half, creating an artificial distinction between economic and noneconomic rights, with only the latter being afforded the status of fundamental rights (Dorn 1986). As Mayer (2011: 8) notes, "It is the creation of this double standard, under which economic liberty and property rights are devalued compared with more favored liberty rights, that improper judicial activism ... can truly be found."

[...]

In the modern redistributive state, equality of rights has been crowded out by equality of outcome; equal opportunity has been turned on its head; and limited government has given way to legislative activism. Cronyism and rent seeking have become the dominant features of democratic states as special interests seek to use the power of government for their own benefit. Consequently, the constitutional perspective—with its emphasis on ordered liberty, equal rights, and a just rule of law—has been seriously eroded.[1] Accordingly, **the security of private property and freedom of contract have been jeopardized with a consequent rise in the uncertainty surrounding rights to property, liberty, and contract.**

Equality of Rights and the Constitution of Liberty

From a constitutional perspective, equality means first and foremost the equality of rights under a just rule of law, with the basic right of every individual being the right to noninterference (Pilon 1979b, 1979c, 1981, 1983). That fundamental right stands at the center of what F. A. Hayek (1960) called the "constitution of liberty."

The basic principles inherent in the natural rights doctrine were stated in the Declaration of Independence and were used to justify the American Revolution. Their content is well-known: "All men are created equal … with certain unalienable Rights"; "to secure these rights, Governments are instituted among Men, deriving their just powers from the consent of the governed"; and "whenever any Form of Government becomes destructive of these ends, it is the Right of the People to alter or abolish it." The Constitution stands on those higher-law principles and is best viewed as a charter for limited government and individual freedom, not a blueprint for majority rule (see, e.g., Barnett 2004, Neily 2013).

The higher-law standing behind the written Constitution is what Cicero called "true law"—namely, "right reason, harmonious with nature, diffused among all, constant, eternal; a law which calls to duty by its commands and restrains from evil by its prohibitions" (Corwin 1955: 10). It encompasses the principles inherent in "the rule of law" regarded as "a meta-legal doctrine or a political ideal" (Hayek 1960: 206). Chief among those principles are the supremacy of private or common law, equality of the law, and priority of individual rights (Dicey [1915] 1982: 120–21). Those principles form a common web because equality, justice, and freedom are all central to the higher-law background of the Framers' Constitution.

At the heart of the English common or private law, and implicit in the U.S. Constitution, is what Hume ([1739–40] 1978: 526) called the "three fundamental laws of nature—that of the stability of possession, of its transference by consent, and of the performance of promises." Adam Smith ([1759] 1976: 163) referred to them as the "laws of justice," and F. A. Hayek (1982, vol. 2: 40) termed them the "rules of just conduct." Equality under the law requires equal treatment or due process and, at a more fundamental level, equal rights. Thus, the rule of law places substance above process

James Madison, the chief architect of the Constitution and Bill of Rights, accepted John Locke's natural rights' position that "the *State of Nature* has a Law of Nature to govern it, which obliges every one. And Reason, which is that Law, teaches all Mankind … that being all equal and independent, no one ought to harm another in his Life, Health, Liberty, or Possessions" (Locke 1965: 311). He also accepted Locke's dictum that "The great and *chief end* … of Mens uniting into Commonwealths, and putting themselves under Government, *is the Preservation of their Property,*" by which Locke meant their "Lives, Liberties, and Estates" (p. 395).

Madison, following in the Lockean natural rights tradition, placed property and equality of rights at the core of his constitutional system, a system in which both economic and noneconomic liberties were to be afforded equal protection under the law of the Constitution and enforced by a vigilant judiciary.[2] As Madison (1865: 51) wrote:

> It is sufficiently obvious, that persons and property are the two great subjects on which Governments are to act; and that the rights of persons, and the rights of property, are the objects, for the protection of which Government was instituted. These rights cannot well be separated. The personal right to acquire property, which is a natural right, gives to property, when acquired, a right to protection, as a social right.

In his famous essay "Property," which appeared in the *National Gazette* on March 29, 1793, Madison argued that "in its larger and juster meaning," property "embraces every thing to which a man may attach a value and have a right, and *which leaves to every one else the like advantage*." An individual thus has a property right in "his opinions and the free communication of them, ... in the safety and liberty of his person, ... [and] in the free use of his faculties and free choice of the objects on which to employ them." Justice requires that government safeguard "property of every sort." Consequently, Madison stated: "that alone is a *just* government, which *impartially* secures to every man, whatever is his *own*" (Hunt 1906: 101–2).

[...]

In the Madisonian, natural-rights view of the constitutional contract, there are no welfare rights entailing positive obligations on the part of the state to take private property from A, in the name of "social justice," and redistribute it to B without A's consent. The right to noninterference carries only the negative obligation to refrain from interfering with the equal rights of others to their property and freedom. As such, under the constitution of liberty, there is a consistent set of rights, all of which flow from the basic right to noninterference. In that "world of consistent rights, everyone can enjoy whichever of his rights he chooses to enjoy at the same time and in the same respect that everyone else does, and the negative obligations correlative to these rights can be satisfied by everyone at the same time and in the same respect that he enjoys his own rights by noninterference" (Pilon 1979c: 1340–41).

[...]

Underlying the legitimacy of the Framers' Constitution, therefore, is what John O'Sullivan, editor of the *United States Magazine and Democratic Review*, referred to as the "voluntary principle." In 1837, he wrote: "The best government is that which governs least." Thus, legislation "should be confined to the administration of justice, for the protection of the natural equal rights of the citizen, and the preservation of the social order. In all

Financial Elites Have a Disproportionate Effect on US Government Policy

A 2014 study published in Perspectives on Politics, "Testing Theories of American Politics: Elites, Interest Groups, and Average Citizens," analyzes the relative influence of political actors on policymaking. The researchers sought to better understand the impact of elites, interest groups and voters on the passing of public policies. The authors, Martin Gilens of Princeton and Benjamin Page of Northwestern, based their research on a database of voters' and interest groups' positions on 1,779 issues between 1981 and 2002, and how those positions were or weren't reflected in policy decisions.

The scholars use the data to examine four theoretical conceptions of how American politics works and the degree of influence that parties have on the decision-making process: (1) majoritarian electoral democracy, in which average citizens lead the decision-making process; (2) economic-elite domination; (2) majoritarian pluralism, in which mass-based interest groups provide the driving force; and (4) biased pluralism, where the opinions of business-oriented interest groups weigh most heavily.

"The central point that emerges from our research is that economic elites and organized groups representing business interests have substantial independent impacts on U.S. government policy, while mass-based interest groups and average citizens have little or no independent influence," the scholars conclude, providing "substantial support" for the theories of economic-elite domination and biased pluralism.

"The influence of elites, interest groups and average voters on American politics," by Martin Maximino, Journalist's Resource, November 14, 2014.

respects, the voluntary principle, the principle of freedom … affords the true golden rule" (Vernier 1987: 12). From a constitutional perspective, then, equality refers to the equal rights of individuals to be free from interferences affecting their lives, liberties, and estates.

Buchanan and Tullock, in their classic *Calculus of Consent* (1962: 250), argue that when choosing the rules of the game (the constitution) "full consensus ... among all members of the social group seems ... to be the only conceivable test of the 'rightness' of the choices made."[3] Indeed, it is the *voluntary* nature of any choice that justifies it under the process-driven model, but one must also ask if anyone's rights have been violated in the process. Hence, in determining the legitimacy of governments, "process will not carry the day; substance must" (Pilon 1985: 826). That is why the rights-driven model of constitutional legitimacy is a necessary complement to the unanimity rule. By accepting property, liberty, and contract as self-evident natural rights, the Framers' sought a system of government that would secure those rights.

In sum, individual rights to life, liberty, and property are justified by "right reason" not by majoritarianism, and the function of a just government is to protect both economic and noneconomic rights under the rubric of the property right. In this sense, Pilon (1985: 829) emphasizes that the "substantive element [in due process] is justified not because it reflects the will of the majority, not because it has been determined by some democratic process, but because it is derived from principles of reason."

[...]

Endnotes

1. The institution of slavery cast a big shadow on the Framers' Constitution, though the Civil War amendments helped to rectify that injustice. The "constitutional perspective" is one that recognizes fundamental rights and the importance of just rules that guide long-run behavior so that individual actions can be coordinated and result in economic and social harmony. That is why well-defined property rights are so important.
2. For an in-depth account of the higher-law background of the Constitution and its influence on Madison, as well as his view of the judiciary, see Dorn (1988).
3. Rutledge Vining, who influenced Buchanan and Tullock at the University of Virginia, recognized this aspect when he wrote: "To be free to act as one chooses and at the same time to recognize the freedom of others to do likewise can only mean that all participate equally in setting the constraints upon individual action. For no one is free unless all abide by the rules of conduct which all can be brought to accept as approximate constraints upon individual action.... To require of each individual that he takes no action which impairs the freedom of any other individual is to accept the moral principle that no individual should treat another simply as a means to an end. Each individual chooses the rules and principles for the guidance of his conduct, but he does so under the general principle that no rule of action will be adopted which could not be universally adopted by all individuals [Vining 1956: 18–19]."

Viewpoint 3

"Today, this old problem of citizen ignorance and its political role has been worsened by the expansion of the scale and scope of the federal government and its agencies over the last 75 years.

Smaller Governments Require Less-Informed Citizens

Bruce Thornton

In the following viewpoint, Bruce Thornton argues that the idea that only smart, well-informed people are capable of being good citizens in democracies goes back as far as ancient Athens. However, the US founding fathers didn't trust the elite with power any more than they trusted the uneducated masses, he points out, so that is why they devised a system with a balance of powers in which each branch of government has checks and balances on the others. Modern society and modern government have brought the problem to the fore again, however, and the author suggests that smaller government may be the answer. Thornton is a fellow at the Hoover Institute and a professor of classics at California State University.

As you read, consider the following questions:

1. Why, according to this viewpoint, do citizens of modern democracies need to be better-informed than citizens in the past?
2. Does Thornton find the pattern of "contempt" for the masses justifiable?
3. What solutions to this problem have been suggested before, according to this article?

In December, MIT Professor Jonathan Gruber, one of the architects of the Affordable Care Act, had to explain to Congress several remarks he had made about the "stupidity of the American voter," as he put it in one speech. Conservative radio host Rush Limbaugh frequently uses the more diplomatic phrase "low-information voter" to explain why bad policies or incompetent politicians succeed. And numerous polls of respondents' knowledge of history and current events repeatedly imply the same conclusion—that the American people are not informed or smart enough for democracy.

This bipartisan disdain for the masses has been a constant theme of political philosophy for over 2,500 years. From the beginnings of popular rule in ancient Athens, the competence of the average person to manage the state has been called into question by critics of democracy. Lacking the innate intelligence or the acquired learning necessary for dispassionately judging policy, the masses instead are driven by their passions or private short-term interests.

The earliest critic of democracy, an Athenian known as the Old Oligarch, wrote that "among the common people are the greatest ignorance, ill-discipline, and depravity." Aristotle argued that the need to make a living prevents most people from acquiring the education and developing the virtues necessary for running the state. He said the "best form of state will not admit them to citizenship." And Socrates famously sneered at the notion that any "tinker, cobbler, sailor, passenger; rich and poor, high and low" could be consulted on "an affair of state."

By the time of the Constitutional convention in 1787, this distrust of the masses had long been a staple of political philosophy. Roger Sherman, a lawyer and future Senator from Massachusetts, who opposed letting the people directly elect members of the House of Representatives, typified the antidemocratic sentiment of many delegates. He argued that the people "should have as little to do as may be about the government," for "they want information and are constantly liable to be misled."

Most of the delegates in Philadelphia were not quite as wary as Sherman of giving the people too much direct power, but in the end they allowed them to elect directly only the House of Representatives. Such sentiments were also frequently heard in the state conventions that ratified the Constitution, where the antifederalists' charge of a "democracy deficit" in the Constitution were met with protestations that the document was designed to protect, as John Dickinson of Delaware put it, "the worthy against the licentious," the men of position, education, and property against the volatile, ignorant masses.

Unlike earlier antidemocrats, however, the framers of the Constitution did not believe that a Platonic elite superior by birth, wealth, or learning could be trusted with unlimited political power, since human frailty and depravity were universal, and power was of "an encroaching nature," as George Washington said, prone to expansion and corruption. Hence the Constitution dispersed power among the three branches of government, so that each could check and balance the other. For as Alexander Hamilton said, "Give all power to the many, they will oppress the few. Give all power to the few they will oppress the many. Both therefore ought to have power, that each may defend itself against the other."

A century later, for all its talk of expanding democracy, the Progressive movement of the late nineteenth and early twentieth centuries promoted a form of rule by elites, dismissing the fear of concentrated power that motivated the founders. The Progressives argued that government by experts was made necessary by industrial capitalism and new transportation and communication technologies, and that the new "sciences" of psychology and sociology were providing knowledge that could guide these technocrats in creating social and economic progress.

Future Progressive president Woodrow Wilson in 1887 argued for this expansion and centralization of federal power in order to form a cadre of administrative elites who, armed with new scientific knowledge about human behavior, could address the novel "cares and responsibilities which will require not a little wisdom, knowledge, and experience," as he wrote in his essay "The Study of Administration." This administrative power, Wilson went on, should be insulated from politics, just as other technical knowledge like engineering or medicine was not accountable to the approval of voters. Thus Wilson envisioned federal bureaucracies "of skilled, economical administration" comprising the "hundred who are wise" empowered to guide the "thousands" who are "selfish, ignorant, timid, stubborn, or foolish."

Like the antidemocrats going back to ancient Athens, Wilson's ideas reflected contempt for the people who lack this specialized knowledge and so cannot be trusted with the power to run their own lives. Today's progressives, as Jonathan Gruber's remarks show, share the same distrust of the masses and the preference for what French political philosopher Chantal Delsol calls "techno-politics," rule by technocrats.

Thus on coming into office in 2009, President Obama said that on issues like stem-cell research or climate change, he aimed "to develop a strategy for restoring scientific integrity to government decision-making" and to protect them from politics. We hear the same technocratic ideal in one of Hillary Clinton's favorite talking points, that public policy should be guided by "evidence-based decision making" rather than by principle, fidelity to the Constitution, or virtue. The important question, however, is whether or not political decision-making requires technical knowledge more than the wisdom gleaned from experience, mores, and morals.

Today, this old problem of citizen ignorance and its political role has been worsened by the expansion of the scale and scope of the federal government and its agencies over the last 75 years. Indeed, the complexity of the policies that federal agencies enforce and manage has made Wilson's ideas about the necessity for government by technocratic elites a self-fulfilling prophecy. In 1960, economist F. A. Hayek made this point about the Social Security program, noting that "the ordinary economist or sociologist or lawyer is today nearly as ignorant [as the layman] of the details of that complex and ever changing system."

This makes the champions and managers of such programs the "experts" whom citizens and Congressmen must trust, and these unelected, unaccountable "experts" are "almost by definition, persons who are in favor of the principles underlying the policy." This problem has obviously been magnified by the exponential growth of federal agencies and programs since 1960, the workings of which few people, including most Congressmen, understand.

If we accept, as many do today, that governing is a matter of technical knowledge, then the lack of knowledge among the masses is a problem, given that politicians are accountable to the voters on Election Day. If, however, politics is a question of principle and common sense, the wisdom of daily life necessary for humans to get along and cooperate with one another, then technical knowledge is not as important as those other qualities.

This is the argument made by an early champion of democracy, the philosopher Protagoras, a contemporary of Socrates. Protagoras defended democracy by pointing out that Zeus gave *all* humans "reverence and justice to be the ordering principles of cities and the bonds of friendship and conciliation." Political communities could not even exist if "virtues" and "justice and wisdom" were not the birthright of all people. As such, as James Madison wrote in 1792, "mankind are capable of governing themselves" and of understanding "the general interest of the community," and so should not be subjected to elites, whether defined by birth, wealth, or superior knowledge, which have "debauched themselves into a persuasion that mankind are incapable of governing themselves."

A big government comprising numerous programs whose workings and structure are obscure to most people has indeed made citizen ignorance a problem. In his detailed analysis of polls taken during the 2012 presidential election, political philosopher Ilya Somin writes in his book *Democracy and Political Ignorance*, "Voters are ignorant not just about specific policy issues but about the structure of government and how it operates," as well as "such basic aspects of the U.S. political system as who has the power to declare war, the respective functions of the three branches of government, and who controls monetary policy."

Though many critics from both political parties complain about this ignorance among the citizenry, solutions generally involve wholesale, and unlikely, transformations of social institutions, like reforming school curricula or correcting the ideological biases of the media.

As Somin points out, however, the modern problem of citizen ignorance is in fact an argument for a much more important reform--a return to the limited central government enshrined in the Constitution. State governments should be the highest level of governmental policy except for those responsibilities Constitutionally entrusted to the federal government, such as foreign policy, securing the national borders, and overseeing interstate commerce. On all else, the principle of subsidiarity should apply--decision-making should devolve to the lowest practical level, as close as possible to those who will be affected by it. The closer to the daily lives and specific social and economic conditions of the voters, the more likely they are to have the knowledge necessary for political deliberation and choice. In this way the cultural, economic, and regional diversity of the country will be respected. And it will be much easier for citizens to acquire the information necessary for deliberating and deciding on issues that impact their lives.

Shrinking the federal government may sound as utopian as transforming our schools or restoring journalistic integrity. The difference, however, is that the federal government and its entitlement programs need money, and our $18 trillion debt, trillion-dollar deficits, and $130 trillion in unfunded liabilities are unsustainable. Sooner or later the time will come when a smaller federal government will be imposed on us by necessity. Perhaps then we will rediscover the wisdom that the smaller the government, the easier it is for us to have enough knowledge to manage it.

Viewpoint 4

> *"There are numerous historical cases where American voters committed terrible mistakes in large part because of political ignorance."*

Uninformed Voters Weaken Democracy

Ilya Somin

In the previous viewpoint, the author argued that smaller government was the answer to the ignorance of the voting population. Writer Ilya Somin takes a different tack. In the following viewpoint, Somin writes a response to another writer, Sean Trende, who argued that political ignorance was not so big a problem as some have suggested. Somin argues that while uninformed voters do make good decisions in some cases, lack of voter knowledge weakens a democracy. Somin is a professor of law at George Mason University in Fairfax, Virginia.

As you read, consider the following questions:

1. What examples does the author give of situations in which a majority of the public misunderstood key issues?
2. What is the "binary choice fallacy" as explained in this viewpoint?
3. What issues in the nation's history does Somin believe would have been supported earlier by more people had the population been better informed?

"Do Voters Know Enough to Make Good Decisions on Important Issues? Reply to Sean Trende," by Ilya Somin, Cato Unbound, October 2013. Reprinted by permission.

I would like to thank Sean Trende for his kind words and thoughtful analysis. Sean offers three important criticisms of the argument advanced in *Democracy and Political Ignorance*: that voters know enough to make good decisions on really important issues, that they can make good choices between the two options on offer in major elections, and that the historical success of American democracy suggests that political ignorance may not be such a serious problem. Each of these points has some merit. But each is overstated. Political ignorance does not prevent voters from making good decisions in some important situations. But it does make the performance of democracy a lot worse than it would be otherwise.

Voter Knowledge on the Big Issues

Sean emphasizes that even if voters are often ignorant, they usually at least understand the big issues in an election. This is sometimes true, but far less often than he supposes. For example, Sean cites the 2010 midterm election as one where the voters were well-informed about big issues. According to the majority of Americans at the time, the most important issue was the state of the economy. Yet preelection polls showed that 67% of voters did not even realize that the economy had grown rather than shrunk during the previous year. The majority also did not know the basics of the 2009 stimulus bill, the most important policy adopted by the Obama administration to try to promote economic recovery. Moreover, a plurality believed that the 2008 bailout of major banks enacted to try to contain the financial crisis and recession that occurred that year – had been enacted under Obama rather than under President George W. Bush (only 34% knew the correct answer).[1]

As Sean notes, over 70% of the public in 2010 did know that Congress had recently passed a health care reform law. But polls throughout 2009 and 2010 repeatedly showed that most of the public had little understanding of what was actually included in that law. As I noted in my lead essay, extensive public ignorance about Obamacare persists to this day, even though it has been a high-profile political issue for years. Knowing that Congress has passed a health care reform law is only of very limited utility if you don't know what the law does. This kind of ignorance about major issues was far from unique to 2010. There was comparable ignorance in numerous other elections, some of which I discuss in detail in the book.

In addition, ignorance sometimes dictates what voters consider to be important issues in the first place. For example, as I noted in the lead essay, most of the public greatly underestimates the percentage of federal spending that goes to entitlement programs, while overestimating that which goes to foreign aid. A public better-informed on these issues would likely put a higher priority on entitlement reform.

Voters don't always get every issue wrong. To the contrary, they do get some important things right, especially if the issue is relatively simple and if the incumbents have committed some major error whose effects are obvious even to relatively ignorant voters. One such case, noted by Sean, was the onset of the Great Depression in the early 1930s, when the voters justifiably punished Herbert Hoover and the Republican Party for their poor performance. But even in that instance, voter ignorance then led the public to support a number of severely misguided policies over the next few years, including the cartelization of much of the economy in ways that raised prices for the poor and increased unemployment relative to what they would have been otherwise. And in most cases, the relative success or failure of the incumbent party is much less glaring than it was in 1932.

Sean is right that some issues are complicated enough that even highly knowledgeable voters are likely to make mistakes. But knowing basic facts about the issues is likely to at least reduce the error rate substantially, even if it cannot eliminate all errors. Moreover, on many issues the public persists in serious errors that the vast majority of knowledgeable experts on both sides of the political spectrum condemn. For example, economists overwhelmingly agree that free trade is good for the economy, yet the majority of the public consistently believes otherwise. Similarly, both liberal and conservative economists oppose our massive system of farm subsidies, which mostly reward large agribusinesses. Yet these subsidies persist and grow, in part because much of the public is unaware of what they do, and in part because majority opinion believes that we might experience food shortages without them.

The Binary Choice Fallacy

Sean also argues that voters only need sufficient knowledge to make good choices between the options put before them by the major parties. In the book, I call this commonly advanced argument the "binary choice fallacy," because it relies on the false assumption that all voters do is choose between two preset alternatives. As I spelled out more fully in my response to Heather Gerken, the argument is a fallacy because the candidates and platforms put forward by the major parties are themselves heavily influenced by voter ignorance. If the public were more knowledgeable, the parties would have strong incentives to put forward better candidates and policies.

Even in their choices between the candidates and parties actually on offer in particular elections, I am less confident than Sean that the electorate usually makes the right decision. I don't have the time and space get into the relative merits of specific elections and candidates. But, at the very least, the wisdom of many of the public's binary decisions in recent elections is far from clear.

Like some other scholars, Sean suggests that, even if many voters are ignorant, the mistakes of the ignorant will cancel each other out, thereby allowing more knowledgeable voters to determine electoral outcomes. This is a theoretically possible result. But, it rarely happens in practice. In reality, the effects of ignorance are usually not random, but systematic. On a host of issues—including major economic and social policy questions – the views of relatively more informed voters are hugely different from those of relatively ignorant ones, even after controlling for other relevant variables, such as age, race, sex, and partisan identification.[2]

Political Ignorance in American History

Sean's most far-reaching claim is that the relative historic success of the United States suggests that voter ignorance is not such a big problem. This raises so many major issues that I can't even begin to do justice to them in a brief post. But here are a few relevant points.

In calling the United States successful, we have to ask, "relative to what?" The answer, of course, is relative to other nations, nearly all of which are either democracies that also suffer form problems caused by political ignorance, or dictatorships. I do not deny that dictatorships are, on average, much worse than democracies.[3] But the relative superiority of the United States compared to dictatorships and most other democracies is not relevant to the issue I raise in the book: whether democracies would suffer less damage from political ignorance if they limited and decentralized their governments more than they do at present.

During most of its history, the U.S. government was both more limited and more decentralized than most other democracies. The large size, limited central government, and numerous diverse jurisdictions of the United States gave Americans numerous opportunities to vote with their feet. And the informational superiority of foot voting over ballot box voting is, of course, a central thesis of my book. Extensive opportunities for foot voting, rather than ballot box voting, historically made the United States unusual.

Despite America's relative success, there are numerous historical cases where American voters committed terrible mistakes in large part because of political ignorance. For many decades, the majority of white Americans supported first slavery and later segregation in part because they were badly misguided in their views of the likely consequences of giving blacks equal rights. More recently, public ignorance about the nature of homosexuality was a major factor in promoting widespread discrimination against gays and lesbians.

Ignorance of basic economics contributed to public support for numerous protectionist laws, including the Smoot-Hawley Tariff, which significantly exacerbated the Great Depression. These and other well-known examples merely scratch the surface. Scholars have only begun to document the historical impact of voter ignorance on public policy.

Sean could point out, correctly, that many of these ignorance-induced policies enjoyed substantial support among knowledgeable elites as well. However, in nearly all of the cases where we have relevant survey data, more knowledgeable people were significantly less likely to support harmful policies. Survey data going back to the 1930s and 40s shows that more knowledgeable whites were more likely to be racially tolerant. In recent decades, more knowledgeable heterosexuals have been more tolerant of gays and lesbians. Knowledgeable voters are also more likely to oppose protectionism, and they have been for decades. If we had better data on 19th century public opinion, I strongly suspect that more knowledgeable voters would have been more likely to, for example, support abolitionism and equal rights for women. In these and many other cases, a more knowledgeable electorate would likely have made fewer egregious errors and corrected those it did make faster.

In sum, it is certainly true that an ignorant electorate can still sometimes make good decisions. But all too often, widespread voter ignorance is *not* good enough for government work.

Notes

1. For data on these three instances of political ignorance in 2010, see Ilya Somin, *Democracy and Political Ignorance: Why Smaller Government is Smarter* (Stanford: Stanford University Press, 2013), 22
2. I criticize this and other "miracle of aggregation" arguments in much greater detail in the book. See ibid., pp. 109-17.
3. Ibid., 8-9, 103-04.

Viewpoint 5

"No other democracy in the world has a system quite like this, a system in which the legislative branch is regularly up for grabs in an election in which the executive branch is not."

The US System of Government Virtually Guarantees Low Voter Turnout

Eric Black

In the following viewpoint, Eric Black contends that voter turnout in the United States swings from bad to worse and back to bad. Black argues that the US Constitutional system, which is designed to keep a balance among the branches of government and prevent short-term swings in public opinion from making unintended and long-term changes to policy, has inadvertently created a government in which voter turnout is typically low. Citizens have assured themselves that because the system is designed to correct itself, stability is assured and nothing calamitous could happen. This false sense of security is a threat to democracy. Black is a political columnist for MinnPost.

"Why do so few citizens participate in our democracy?" by Eric Black, MinnPost, September 29, 2014. Reprinted by permission.

As you read, consider the following questions:

1. In what way does this author say that the US system is built for gridlock?
2. How does Black judge the health of a democracy?
3. Why, according to Black, did the framers of the US Constitution stagger elections?

On the one hand, I assume that most Americans (myself included) believe that the United States, since the founding, has been a generally positive force and an example for the idea of democracy, the development of democracy, the promotion of democracy, and (even in spite of many historical deviations from that generalization) we are mostly proud of that in some gauzy, inchoate way that links up with both our patriotism and our national vanity.

On the other hand, in 1958, when pollsters first asked Americans whether they trusted the government to do the right thing, 73 percent said "yes," "just about always" or at least "most of the time." In 2010 that number was down to 22 percent. (Although, not to awfulize overmuch, by 2013, with the improvement in the economy, it had bumped back up to 26 percent.) The National Election Survey, which created that question, developed a slightly more complicated "Trust in Government Index," but it makes the same point.

At the moment, we have a president, chosen twice by us for that (hard, thankless) job, whose approval ratings long since fell below 50 percent and keep reaching new lows. On the third hand, approval of President Obama looks positively stratospheric compared to the approval ratings of Congress, at least collectively. And since, at least according to the theory, We the People elected all these folks we dislike, distrust and disapprove of, the question might be raised what kind of approval rating We the People give to We the People when we look (figuratively and collectively) in a very large mirror.

Or is it the system?

It's an election year here in the nation that considers itself the capital of world democracy, and a reasonable occasion for considering those questions. Collectively, theoretically at least, we have an opportunity to change some of the things that are bothering us. But, strangely, there doesn't seem to be much real, consequential change on the ballot. The pundits think it's somewhat likely that, after the election, partisan control of the U.S. Senate will have flipped from Democrats to Republicans. But with Obama still in the White House, it seems likely that some form of gridlock will continue in a Washington that has mostly forgotten how to compromise across party lines.

But that conundrum is mostly about the constitutional system of government, as evolved, which is in many respects built for gridlock. I wrote that series in the last election year. This time, I want to focus on issues of campaigning and especially voting. My plan is to look at some of the troubling indicators that our way of doing democracy is not delivering all the democracy it should or could, and then to look around the world, and talk to political scientists who specialize in those kinds of international comparisons of democracies and see what we can figure out.

I hope the series will be an invitation to the open-minded to set aside our (possibly overweening) pride in America's system of democracy and consider whether we can learn anything from the rest of the democratic world, as the rest of the democratic world has learned much from our example, including, in some cases, what not to do.

Many relatively recent comers to the world of democracy have benefited from our older experiment, but few of them decide to adopt our system. They have the benefit of our experience and can look for ways to avoid our mistakes.

The idea of my little exercise of comparative democracy is to reverse the favor by looking at aspects of democracy that may be working better elsewhere and see if they have figured out any tricks worth emulating or even just considering.

Citizen Participation

How do you measure the health of a democracy? One obvious and absolutely valid first thought is to measure the level of citizen participation, and the basic form of such participation is voting.

Of all the developed democracies in the world, the United States ranks near the bottom in the portion of its voting-age citizen population that votes. And, I'm afraid to tell you, the situation is even worse than that general statement makes it look.

"A Different Democracy: American Government in a 31-Country Perspective," a soon-to-be published text on comparative democracy, examines U.S. democracy in the context of (you guessed it) 31 developed democracies across the six populated continents of the world (although the biggest chunk of the 31 are in Europe). The lead author, political scientist Steven Taylor of Troy University in Alabama, kindly shared with me an advance copy of the chapter that deals with voter turnout.

It includes a chart depicting the percentage of the voting-age population that actually voted in all 31 democracies in the period 1990-2010. The highest turnout is Italy, with an average participation rate of 86.12 percent. The top 10 countries by this measure — all with average turnouts above 78 percent — are Italy, Belgium, Greece, Australia, Denmark, Sweden, Brazil, Finland, Korea and New Zealand.

The United States comes in 29th of the 31 nations, with an average turnout of 57.28 percent.

That is a bad number. Very bad. You can argue, I suppose, that as long as people have a right to vote, it is up to them whether they choose to exercise that right. I'm not interested in making excuses for lazy or tuned-out voters, but Professor Bingham Powell of the University of Rochester, a veteran comparer of different systems of democracy, urges me (and you) to bear in mind that "lots of things affect voter turnout other than interest and competence of the voters."

Even bearing that mind, in judging the health of a democracy, I don't know how a low rate of voting participation can be taken as anything other than a serious sign of democratic ill health.

It Gets Worse...

Some of those "other" factors will be the subject of the next installment, but first allow me to argue that the U.S. turnout is actually quite a bit worse than that 57 percent participation rate makes it look.

Because this is 2014, it's a midterm election year, as you know. The bad number above is the average of five presidential elections. And presidential elections always have a substantially larger turnout than any other in the U.S. election cycle.

Curtis Gans of the Center for the Study of the American Electorate, who specializes in studying turnout, says that presidential election turnouts in recent history have been generally in the upper 50s, occasionally breaking into the low 60s, and midterm turnouts have fairly consistently hovered just above and below the 40 percent mark. Here are Gans' calculations of the turnouts over the last five midterm elections:

- 1994: 40.9 percent
- 1998: 37.9 percent
- 2002: 39.6 percent
- 2006: 40.6 percent
- 2010: 41.5 percent

As you can see, there's been a slight uptick over the last few cycles, but Gans believes this trend is ending. After studying turnout in the primaries so far this cycle (it hit a record low in 15 of the first 25 states to hold primaries this year), Gans is projecting a drop in the turnout on Election Day this year from the level of recent midterms.

When constructing the table that ranked the United States 29th out of 31 democracies in turnout, the authors of the textbook cited above rated each country according to the highest-turnout election in its normal cycle. But nobody else on the list has a system that alternates regularly between a high-turnout election and a low-turnout election. In a typical election elsewhere in the democratic world, everything is on table.

So let's just look this square in the face. It's true that the presidency is not on the ballot this year. And that makes the midterm a somewhat less important election. But all 435 seats in the U.S. House of Representatives and 35 Senate seats, including the one in Minnesota (there's a couple of extras because of vacancies), will be on the ballot.

Theoretically, this is an opportunity for the electorate to deeply change the power structure in Washington, and to send, in the most meaningful and democratic way, a signal about what they want their national government to do over the next two years. It's somewhat unlikely that this election will result in such a clear signal. But even if it does, the message will be sent by just 40 percent of the voting-age population.

We're Different

No other democracy in the world has a system quite like this, a system in which the legislative branch is regularly up for grabs in an election in which the executive branch is not. A system in which we have alternating turnouts from bad (60 percent) to worse (40 percent) then back to bad then back to worse.

You can say this was in a sense part of the Framers' design. They built the staggered terms into the U.S. Constitution. There is general agreement that they wanted to cushion the national government from short-term swings in public opinion, and to make a bit harder to change the whole government with one sudden gust of public opinion that might be short-lived.

But the Framers did not mean to set up this weird alternation between bad and worse turnouts. It was not anyone's intention and it's hard to imagine why anyone would ever intend such a pattern. It has just evolved. And it's pretty crazy. And no other democracy in the world has anything like that going on.

Periodical and Internet Sources Bibliography

The following articles have been selected to supplement the diverse views presented in this chapter.

Russell Berman, "How Can the US Shrink the Influence of Money in Politics?" *Atlantic*, March 16, 2016. https://www.theatlantic.com/politics/archive/2016/03/fix-money-in-politics/473214.

Carl Bialik, "Voter Turnout Fell, Especially in the States that Clinton Won," Fivethirtyeight, November 11, 2016. https://fivethirtyeight.com/features/voter-turnout-fell-especially-in-states-that-clinton-won.

David Brooks, "The Crisis of Western Civ," *New York Times*, April 21, 2017. https://www.nytimes.com/2017/04/21/opinion/the-crisis-of-western-civ.html?mtrref=undefined&assetType=opinion&mtrref=www.nytimes.com&gwh=5623291F6EAFB22A4696854D43279E59&gwt=pay&assetType=opinion.

David Cole, "How to Reverse Citizens United: What Campaign Finance Reformers Can Learn from the NRA," *Atlantic*, April 2016. https://www.theatlantic.com/magazine/archive/2016/04/how-to-reverse-citizens-united/471504.

David French, "Stop the Hysterics over 'Voter Suppression,'" *National Review*, November 2, 2016. http://www.nationalreview.com/article/441698/voter-suppression-not-selma-stop-hysterics.

Mark Joseph Stern, "America Is Already in the Midst of a Voter Suppression Crisis: We Didn't Even Need to Wait for Election Day," Slate, October 31, 2016. http://www.slate.com/articles/news_and_politics/jurisprudence/2016/10/republicans_are_already_suppressing_minority_votes_all_over_america.html.

Courtney Subramanian, "US Election: Why Does the US Have Such Low Voter Turnout?" BBC, October 28, 2016. http://www.bbc.com/news/election-us-2016-37634526.

Adam Taylor, "American Voter Turnout Is Still Lower Than Most Other Wealthy Nations," *Washington Post,* November 10, 2016. http://interactive.fusion.net/rise-up-be-heard/voting-participation.html.

Chapter 2

Can Western Democracies Withstand the Recent Trend Toward Authoritarianism?

Chapter Preface

When the totalitarian communist regimes of Eastern Europe began collapsing like dominoes in 1989, many people saw it as the ultimate victory for democracy. But the notion of democracy and authoritarianism facing off against each other like good guys and bad guys in an old Western movie never really made much sense. Authoritarianism, at least according to many experts, is a worm at the heart of all democracies. Now, some three decades after the fall of the Berlin Wall, democracy seems at risk even in places where it has been taken for granted for centuries. What accounts for the recent trend toward authoritarianism in places that were once considered bastions of democracy? And is the democracy in those places strong enough to withstand it?

People are more willing to accept—even be attracted to—strong tyrannical leaders when they feel threatened, either economically or in some other way. Citizens may choose to give up a great deal of freedom in exchange for what they perceive as safety. However, it is not always a conscious trade-off. Authoritarianism, it seems, is something democratic nations slide back into rather than deliberately choose. It is unlikely that very many of the Americans who cast their votes for Donald Trump in 2016 believed that they were trading freedom for protection from terrorism and economic struggles. Yet they nonetheless elected a man who insists that a free press—one of the foundations of a free society—is the "enemy," and who has repeatedly expressed scorn for the Judiciary, one of the three branches of government and the branch with the most power to protect the rights of the individual citizen against the ruthlessness of authoritarian leaders. Most of the voters who supported Marine Le Pen in France, Nigel Farage in the UK, or Geert Wilders in the Netherlands were likely not consciously supporting a return to totalitarianism, but somehow believed that their interests would be represented by these candidates and that they would still retain some control of their societies and their lives. A bit of history might remind them the risk of that kind of thinking.

It is worth noting that Adolf Hitler came to power in Germany in 1933 by democratic elections in a parliamentary system, and then consolidated that power by enacting anti-democratic policies and suppressing dissent and opposition, both in the press and from trade unions, and quite quickly made himself the sole ruler of the nation. This is, of course, not to say that Donald Trump, Marine Le Pen, and other far-right politicians are would-be Hitlers, but simply to point out that authoritarianism doesn't always arrive—at least not at first—in jackboots and tanks. It is quite possible that citizens with mostly benevolent intent can use their votes and influence in such a way as to find themselves ensnared in a totalitarian government that was much easier to install than depose.

In this chapter, you will read viewpoints that examine the trend toward authoritarianism in the West, and particularly in the United States, asking just what conditions lead to deconsolidation of modern democracies and what might be done to reverse that trend, while still respecting the concerns of citizens who do not feel as safe and protected by their governments as they would like.

VIEWPOINT 1

> *"Democracy virtually assures that only bad and dangerous men will ever rise to the top of government."*

The Ability for Anyone to Become President Is One of Democracy's Greatest Weaknesses

Hans-Hermann Hoppe

In the following viewpoint, Hans-Hermann Hoppe argues that the ability of anyone to become president or prime minister is one of the primary flaws of democracy. The author argues that democracies enhance the human tendency to covet the property of others and the opportunity to get away with taking that property. Unlike with a monarchy, he contends, democracy virtually assures that only bad and dangerous men will ever rise to the top of government. Hoppe is a libertarian/anarcho-capitalist philosopher, professor emeritus of economics at University of Nevada Las Vegas, and senior fellow with the Mises Institute, an organization that promotes libertarian thought, privileging private property over the common good.

"Why Democracy Rewards Bad People," by Hans-Hermann Hoppe, Mises Institute, June 10, 2016. Reprinted with the permission of the Mises Institute.

As you read, consider the following questions:

1. How are this author's views of what government is and does different from others you have read?
2. What, according to Hoppe, is the main danger of opening government to everyone?
3. How does or does not the long closing quote support Hoppe's argument?

One of the most widely accepted propositions among political economists is the following: Every monopoly is bad from the viewpoint of consumers. Monopoly is understood in its classical sense to be an exclusive privilege granted to a single producer of a commodity or service, i.e., as the absence of free entry into a particular line of production. In other words, only one agency, A, may produce a given good, x. Any such monopolist is bad for consumers because, shielded from potential new entrants into his area of production, the price of the monopolist's product x will be higher and the quality of x lower than otherwise.

This elementary truth has frequently been invoked as an argument in favor of democratic government as opposed to classical, monarchical or princely government. This is because under democracy entry into the governmental apparatus is free—anyone can become prime minister or president—whereas under monarchy it is restricted to the king and his heir.

However, this argument in favor of democracy is fatally flawed. Free entry is not always good. Free entry and competition in the production of goods is good, but free competition in the production of bads is not. Free entry into the business of torturing and killing innocents, or free competition in counterfeiting or swindling, for instance, is not good; it is worse than bad. So what sort of "business" is government? Answer: it is not a customary producer of goods sold to voluntary consumers. Rather, it is a "business" engaged in theft and expropriation—by means of taxes and counterfeiting—and the fencing of stolen goods. Hence, free entry into government does not improve something good. Indeed, it makes matters worse than bad, i.e., it improves evil.

Since man is as man is, in every society people who covet others' property exist. Some people are more afflicted by this sentiment than others, but individuals usually learn not to act on such feelings or even feel ashamed for entertaining them. Generally only a few individuals are unable to successfully suppress their desire for others' property, and they are treated as criminals by their fellow men and repressed by the threat of physical punishment. Under princely government, only one single person—the prince—can legally act on the desire for another man's property, and it is this which makes him a potential danger and a "bad."

However, a prince is restricted in his redistributive desires because all members of society have learned to regard the taking and redistributing of another man's property as shameful and immoral. Accordingly, they watch a prince's every action with utmost suspicion. In distinct contrast, by opening entry into government, anyone is permitted to freely express his desire for others' property. What formerly was regarded as immoral and accordingly was suppressed is now considered a legitimate sentiment. Everyone may openly covet everyone else's property in the name of democracy; and everyone may act on this desire for another's property, provided that he finds entrance into government. Hence, under democracy everyone becomes a threat.

Consequently, under democratic conditions the popular though immoral and anti-social desire for another man's property is systematically strengthened. Every demand is legitimate if it is proclaimed publicly under the special protection of "freedom of speech." Everything can be said and claimed, and everything is up for grabs. Not even the seemingly most secure private property right is exempt from redistributive demands. Worse, subject to mass elections, those members of society with little or no inhibitions against taking another man's property, that is, habitual a-moralists who are most talented in assembling majorities from a multitude of morally uninhibited and mutually incompatible popular demands (efficient demagogues) will tend to gain entrance in and rise to the top of government. Hence, a bad situation becomes even worse.

Historically, the selection of a prince was through the accident of his noble birth, and his only personal qualification was typically his upbringing as a future prince and preserver of the dynasty, its status, and its possessions. This did not assure that a prince would not be bad and dangerous, of course. However, it is worth remembering that any prince who failed in his primary duty of preserving the dynasty—who ruined the country, caused civil unrest, turmoil and strife, or otherwise endangered the position of the dynasty—faced the immediate risk either of being neutralized or assassinated by another member of his own family. In any case, however, even if the accident of birth and his upbringing did not preclude that a prince might be bad and dangerous, at the same time the accident of a noble birth and a princely education also did not preclude that he might be a harmless dilettante or even a good and moral person.

In contrast, the selection of government rulers by means of popular elections makes it nearly impossible that a good or harmless person could ever rise to the top. Prime ministers and presidents are selected for their proven efficiency as morally uninhibited demagogues. Thus, democracy virtually assures that only bad and dangerous men will ever rise to the top of government. Indeed, as a result of free political competition and selection, those who rise will become increasingly bad and dangerous individuals, yet as temporary and interchangeable caretakers they will only rarely be assassinated.

One can do no better than quote H. L. Mencken in this connection. "Politicians," he notes with his characteristic wit, "seldom if ever get [into public office] by merit alone, at least in democratic states. Sometimes, to be sure, it happens, but only by a kind of miracle. They are chosen normally for quite different reasons, the chief of which is simply their power to impress and enchant the intellectually underprivileged....Will any of them venture to tell the plain truth, the whole truth and nothing but the truth about the situation of the country, foreign or domestic? Will any of them refrain from promises that he knows he can't fulfill—that no human being could fulfill? Will any of them utter a word, however obvious, that will alarm or alienate any of the huge pack of morons who cluster at the public trough, wallowing in the pap that grows thinner and thinner, hoping against hope? Answer: may be for a few weeks at the start.... But not after the issue is fairly joined, and the struggle is on in earnest.... They will all promise every man, woman and child in the country whatever he, she or it wants. They'll all be roving the land looking for chances to make the rich poor, to remedy the irremediable, to succor the unsuccorable, to unscramble the unscrambleable, to dephlogisticate the undephlogisticable. They will all be curing warts by saying words over them, and paying off the national debt with money no one will have to earn. When one of them demonstrates that twice two is five, another will prove that it is six, six and a half, ten, twenty. In brief, they will divest themselves from their character as sensible, candid and truthful men, and simply become candidates for office, bent only on collaring votes. They will all know by then, even supposing that some of them don't know it now, that votes are collared under democracy, not by talking sense but by talking nonsense, and they will apply themselves to the job with a hearty yo-heave-ho. Most of them, before the uproar is over, will actually convince themselves. The winner will be whoever promises the most with the least probability of delivering anything."

Viewpoint 

> *"If Bernie Sanders had been the Democratic Party candidate his 'democratic socialist' platform could have won out against Trump in the presidential election."*

The Democrats Lost in 2016 Because They Did Not Represent the Working Class

Josh Hollands

In the following excerpted viewpoint, Josh Hollands makes the case that the appeal of Donald Trump in the 2016 presidential election was not due to his racist and nativist propaganda, but to the fact that the opposition party had lost touch with the working people it once represented. In contrast to the previous viewpoint, the author argues that demagogues are elected and government stumbles when the powerful do not listen to the voices of the people. When he wrote this piece, Hollands was a PhD candidate at University College London.

"Donald Trump and the US elections," by Josh Hollands, International Socialism, December 17, 2016. Reprinted by permission. This article originally appeared as 'Donald Trump and the US elections' in *International Socialism* 153, January 2017. (http://isj.org.uk/donald-trump-and-the-us-elections/)

As you read, consider the following questions:

1. In what particular way does this author argue that Hillary Clinton was an unsuitable candidate?
2. Why, according to Hollands, did so many working class people fail to vote for either candidate in the 2016 US Presidential Election?
3. How might the Democrats, according to this author, have done better in 2016 if they'd learned more from Bernie Sanders's campaign?

The election of Donald J. Trump as President of the United States of America has rightly been greeted with disgust by many around the world. After a lengthy election season in which the two main parties were led by two of the most unpopular candidates in recent memory the victor was a man who threatens minorities and brags about sexually assaulting women. Wall Street's choice for president, Hillary Clinton, won the popular vote but failed to gain traction in the swing states of Florida, Indiana, North Carolina and Ohio, and lost the Democratic strongholds of Michigan and Wisconsin, therefore falling short of votes in the United States' archaic electoral college. It was in the Northern "rustbelt" states, the area of former industrial strength where car manufacturing, steel production and coal mining have been replaced with low-wage service jobs and crumbling infrastructure, that Trump won by razor-thin margins.

Following the election several narratives have come to dominate among liberals trying to explain why Clinton lost. These range from the idea that white workers were mobilised by misogyny and racism, to there being an "enthusiasm gap" due to the FBI's intervention into Clinton, to arguments that Clinton was the victim of a conspiracy by big business.

[…]

This belies the fact that Clinton was a remarkably unsuitable candidate to inspire working class voters in the US. Earlier in the year the self-proclaimed democratic socialist Bernie Sanders stunned the liberal establishment by winning 22 states and 13 million votes in the Democratic primaries on a platform that included demands for the creation of decent-paying jobs, and the expansion of Medicare and social security among other policies which spoke to their material concerns. Workers in former industrial heartland states such as Michigan and Wisconsin were not going to be pulled towards Clinton, a millionaire seemingly oblivious to the loss of jobs and stagnant wages in Democratic strongholds. Responding to Trump's slogan "make America great again", she told people who have suffered decades of wage stagnation, job losses, and a decline in union organisation that "America is already great". In fact many workers saw a direct link between the neoliberal trade deals championed by Clinton and the decline of their own fortunes, something Trump preyed upon. The election can therefore be seen as a repudiation of the neoliberal consensus that has shaped US capitalism for decades.

Even some on the corporate wing of the Democrats acknowledge that the election result was driven, not by Clinton's claim that the FBI was to blame, but by much more fundamental factors: "Anyone blaming Comey is kidding themselves," said Matt Bennett, co-founder of the Democratic think-tank Third Way (which advocates for the Trans Pacific Partnership trade deal). "It wasn't Comey. It was anger at government and anger at the party of government that she represented and this desire to express this anger as aggressively as possible". Robert Reich, Bill Clinton's one time labor secretary, went even further by arguing: "What happened in America on Election Day should not be seen as a victory for hatefulness over decency. It is more accurately understood as a repudiation of the American power structure, including the old Democratic Party".

Much has been made of Trump's increased share of votes from the "white working class". For years socialists have been told by the mass media that the working class does not exist and yet now we are told that it held the key to the election. The mainstream media have been filled with stories of how impoverished white voters led the charge against the "liberal elite", yet this is overly simplistic.

[...]

The Democratic vote stagnated while Trump managed not only to retain the Republicans' main voting blocks but also to appeal to a minority of voters in former industrial Midwestern states, who had previously pulled the lever for Obama.[3] To simply put this result down to a reactionary working class is too simplistic; the reality is far more complicated. The story is as much about those who did not or could not vote as it is about those who did vote. Some 50 percent of eligible voters did not turn out in the presidential election, a majority of them working class people who felt uninspired by or alienated from the political system.

Michael Moore points out that in some cities, such as Detroit, the turnout to vote on local ballot initiatives was higher than that for the presidential race—some people did go out to vote but could not bring themselves to fill in a box for the presidency for either Trump or Clinton, or a third-party. However, low voter turnout was particularly high in the counties that are poorest and have higher numbers of black voters. New voter identification laws designed to make voting more difficult were introduced this year requiring voters to produce a state-approved ID card before voting, which was particularly difficult for poor voters who are forced to move often. In a June 2013 decision, Shelby County vs Holder, the Supreme Court ruled that "states with a long history of racial discrimination no longer needed to approve any proposed changes to their voting procedures with the federal government, as had long been required under the Voting Rights Act". In practical terms this meant stricter ID laws, limits on opportunities to vote and a reduction in the number of polling stations. As *The New York Times* illustrates: "Milwaukee's lowest-income neighborhoods offer one explanation for the turnout figures. Of the city's 15 council districts, the decline in turnout from 2012 to 2016 in the five poorest was consistently much greater than the drop seen in more prosperous areas—

accounting for half of the overall decline in turnout citywide". In one area, which is 84 percent black, voter turnout declined by a fifth from four years ago. This area also leads in having one of the nation's highest per-capita incarceration rates. As the US *Socialist Worker* points out: "Almost 6 million people can't vote because of state felony disenfranchisement laws. In Florida, almost one in four black adults is disenfranchised". Added to this were those who simply could not bring themselves to vote at all in a year which has seen continued police killings of unarmed civilians and the rise of Black Lives Matter protests. This view was given voice by San Francisco 49ers quarterback Colin Kaepernick, who has supported Black Lives Matter by holding his own protest of kneeling during the pre-game national anthem. He stated that he would not vote because whoever won would be "another face that's going to be the face of that system of oppression".

Why Did Voters Turn to Trump?

What is clear is that while Democratic turnout stagnated in the Midwest, Republican support grew. *The New York Times* writes: "Across the industrial Midwest, white voters who had supported Obama and previous Democrats abandoned the party for Trump". This is important for a number of reasons. First, it shows that white voters did not simply turn to Trump because they were attracted to his racist rhetoric. While racism exists at all levels of society, and part of Trump's position is racist, voters were attracted for predominantly other reasons. Exit polls found that the single most important issue for voters was the state of the US economy, with 52 percent of those asked saying they were most concerned about this. This was far in front of other issues, including terrorism and immigration. As Marxist economist Michael Roberts notes:

> Trump won because he claimed he could improve the conditions of those "who have been left behind" by globalisation, failing domestic industries and crushed small businesses. Of course, Trump is a billionaire and has no real interest or idea about improving the lot of the majority. But anger at the establishment

was sufficient (just) for this egoistic, misogynist, sexual predator, rich man's son to win.

Bernie Sanders's campaign for the Democratic Party nomination highlighted this anger towards the party and for those outside of it. Sanders' success in the Midwestern rustbelt states should have acted as a canary in the coal mine for the Democratic leadership, yet the cabal around the Clintons took these working class votes for granted. Throughout the primary campaign Sanders tapped into the anger of many against the neoliberal elite. He called for the break-up of the largest banks and financial institutions, the creation of decent-paying jobs, equal pay for women, an end to crippling college tuition fees, the expansion of Medicare and social security, for racial justice and action on climate change. Sanders based his campaign on a grassroots approach, soliciting donations of $27 on average. In contrast, Clinton spent her time soliciting donations from entrepreneurs and celebrities. Sanders won the state of Wisconsin by a 13.5 percent margin over Clinton. Yet while Clinton made dozens of trips to California to fundraise among billionaires, she did not set foot in that state after she won the Democratic nomination. It was the crass elitism she represented that made her so uniquely unsuitable to tap into the anger that many felt at the lack of employment opportunities throughout the rustbelt.

That Trump made inroads into these states should not have been that much of a surprise. Trudell noted almost a year ago that: "it is his merging of hysteria over immigration with trade protectionism that is giving him traction". The key point here is trade protectionism. The right in the US has long attacked migrants and sought to scapegoat them for economic crises. What is new is Trump's direct attacks on trade deals such as the North America Free Trade Agreement (NAFTA), that workers have come to blame for low wages, lack of jobs and infrastructure. Trump tapped into a mood that Sanders also spoke to from the left. Robert Reich points out how this has led to a crisis of the Democrats' own making, suggesting that "the Democratic Party once represented the working class. But over the last three decades the party stood by as corporations hammered trade unions, the backbone of the white working class—failing to reform labor laws to impose meaningful penalties on companies that violate them." One might disagree with Reich that the Democrats ever really represented workers but his argument that they have been the ones to damage their own constituents is valid. He notes that union membership fell from 22 percent of all workers in 1992, the year Bill Clinton was elected president, to a pitiful 12 percent today. He also notes: "the working class lost bargaining leverage to get a share of the economy's gains" while inequality continued to widen.

Concerns about jobs, wages and healthcare are not abstract. There have been monumental falls in US living standards with wages stagnating over the past 45 years. Johnson points out that "between 1948 and 1973, productivity rose by 96.7 percent and real wages by 91.3 percent, almost exactly in step... But from 1973 to 2015—the era of globalisation, when many of those jobs vanished abroad—productivity rose 73.4 percent while wages rose by only 11.1 percent." Trump has tapped into the anger around stagnant wages and job losses by playing the age-old tactics of divide and rule arguing that these drops in living standards are caused by migration and globalisation.

Trump's protectionist calls to leave trade deals such as NAFTA and TPP resonated with many. When he appeared in Flint, Michigan, the site of a public health emergency where the city's water supply has been poisoned with lead, Trump linked his protectionist economics with an analogy that spoke to the material concerns of local residents: "It used to be the cars were made in Flint and you couldn't drink the water in Mexico," he said, "Now the cars are built in Mexico and you can't drink the water in Flint", In contrast, Clinton represented the very establishment that introduced NAFTA and threatened to push through the Trans Pacific Partnership (TPP). Whether Trump actually intends to make good on his promises is unclear. What currently matters for understanding how he came to win is that his campaign focused on the economy, voters' chief concern.

[...]

The announcement that Ford was to move small car production from Michigan to Mexico gave further credence to Trump's argument that globalisation was to blame for the lack of work in the Midwest. In a separate episode in Indianapolis Trump specifically called out other firms announcing offshoring. He demanded that the air-conditioning manufacturer Carrier halt its plans to move a factory from the city to Mexico, at a loss of 1,400 jobs. This rhetoric played well into the hands of angry voters who also witnessed jobs in their communities disappearing:

> He cited Carrier again and again on the campaign trail, threatening to phone executives at the company and its parent, United Technologies, and to hit them with 35 percent tariffs on any furnaces and air-conditioners they imported from Mexico. To the cheers of his supporters, he predicted at rallies that Carrier would call him up as president and say, "Sir, we've decided to stay in the United States".

[...]

But the reasons for Trump's success can also be his downfall. The anti-establishment feeling will rapidly fade as he accepts and appoints Washington insiders, the very people he promised to rid by "draining the swamp". Days after his election in November he was already signing insiders up to new roles. Voters who turned on the Democrats for eight years of broken promises on the economy will just as quickly turn on Trump if he fails to deliver on his promises to bring jobs back to the rustbelt: "'If he doesn't pass that tariff, I will vote the other way next time', warned Nicole Hargrove, who has worked at Carrier for a decade and a half and is not certain what she will do if and when her job goes to Mexico".

[...]

If it was the economy that swayed the balance for Trump it will also be his biggest challenge, and possibly his downfall. He now needs to make the economy grow and create jobs in the US while also attacking migrants and unions. Though the US economy's recovery has been better than other large economies since the 2008 financial crash "its economic performance has still been dismal", notes Roberts: "Real GDP growth per person has been only 1.4 percent a year, well below levels before the global financial crash in 2008. It's a story of the weakest economic recovery after a slump since the 1930s". While economists in the US have been confident that a recession is unlikely because housing markets have been strengthening, interest rates have remained low and therefore the cost of borrowing has been at near zero, they have failed to account for the crisis in profitability. As Roberts argues:

> What is important for the health of a modern capitalist economy is not the ease or cost of borrowing, it is the level and direction of the profitability of capital, total business profits and the impact on business investment. When profitability falls, eventually total corporate profits fall and then some time later, business investment will contract. When that happens, an economic recession soon follows…
>
> And US corporate profits are falling. According to economists at investment bank JP Morgan, US corporate profits declined 7 percent over year-ago levels. On that basis, they reckon, "the probability of a recession starting within three years at a startling 92 percent, and the probability within two years at 67 percent".

If such a recession does take place Trump will almost certainly blame it on undocumented workers but these arguments of divide and rule will become harder for him to sell as the fallout from his policies worsens and if resistance is built. The prospects for industrial action in this moment is also strong. Throughout the election year there were bursts of successful strikes suggesting that workers will not take a bosses' offensive lying down. Workers at the communications giant Verizon won major concessions against one of the biggest corporate employers in the US following an all-out strike "in a fight against outsourcing, job losses, pension and healthcare cuts, and wage reductions". Teachers in Chicago have

Occupy Wall Street

Tens of thousands took action Thursday, November 17 to demand that our political system serve all of us—not just the wealthy and powerful. The NYPD estimated tonight's crowd at 32,500 people, at the culmination of the day of action. Thousands more also mobilized in at least 30 cities across the United States. Demonstrations were also held in cities around the world.

New York led the charge in this energizing day for the emerging movement. In the wake of billionaire Mayor Michael Bloomberg's predawn raid of Occupy Wall Street at Liberty Square, 1:00am Tuesday morning, thousands of people throughout the five boroughs and the greater region converged to take peaceful action. Following Bloomberg's action, the slogan "You can't evict an idea whose time has come" became the new meme of the 99% movement overnight. The mobilization today proved that the movement is on the ascent and is capable of navigating obstacles.

"I worked hard and played by the rules, but when budget cuts hit last year I lost my job as an EMT and now I'm about to lose my family's home," said Bronx resident Carlos Rivera. "I'm sitting down on the Brooklyn Bridge today because it's not fair that our taxpayer dollars bailed out big banks like my mortgage holder, Bank of America, but they refuse home-saving loan modifications for struggling families like mine. It's time banks and the super wealthy paid their fair share and Congress helped people get back to work."

"Historic Day of Action for the 99%," OccupyWallSt.org, November 18, 2011

won many of their demands with the threat of a repeat of the all-out industrial action that gripped the city in 2012. Meanwhile, pilots at Amazon's new flight transportation service also threatened a work slow-down over Thanksgiving and Christmas if the company did not provide a better contract for the increased hours they now work. At the same time 1,200 air maintenance workers at the parcel service UPS voted overwhelmingly to strike over pay and healthcare costs. Hundreds of workers at Trump's own properties felt buoyed throughout the campaign to challenge their anti-union, racist boss. On one occasion the Culinary Union organised a wall of taco trucks to surround Trump's Las Vegas hotel in protest at his racist rhetoric and refusal to allow workers to unionise officially. These politicised workers hold the key to pulling down the Trump Presidency and unveiling its true face as an anti-working class charade.

Conclusion

[…]

If Bernie Sanders had been the Democratic Party candidate his "democratic socialist" platform could have won out against Trump in the presidential election. Throughout the primary campaigns he polled considerably better against Trump than Clinton; as demonstrated above, his platform spoke more to those voters who turned their backs on the Democrats as well as independents long put off by both major parties. Those who say he would have lost due to the long aversion to socialism in the US fail to take on board Sanders's success in making socialism no longer a dirty word. If he had broken from the Democrats after the primaries he certainly would have been blamed for Trump's victory but we may also have witnessed the birth of a serious new organisation. Jill Stein's Green Party campaign, supported by many on the socialist left, failed to inspire in the way that Sanders's popular insurgency within the Democrats did. At the same time the liberal narrative of the need to vote for the "lesser-evil" of Clinton clearly did not win among voters who were pulled by both Sanders' and Trump's economic messages in states including Michigan, Wisconsin and Indiana.

[…]

Trump's weakness is that he threatens so many different groups that making connections between them should be easy. The protests that have appeared on the streets since the election, from school students to retirees chanting "We Reject the President-Elect", and plans to march against his inauguration, prove there is already a movement emerging.

[…]

Viewpoint 3

> *"Schools needed to produce well-informed protectors of republican government."*

The Founders Believed Education Was Central to the Government They Had Created

Alan Taylor

In the following viewpoint, Alan Taylor provides historical context to the development of the US system of government and explains the concerns of the founders and the institutions they hoped would protect their young republic. Taylor reminds us of the founding father's original intent to underscore his belief in the importance of an educated public. A knowledgeable citizenry, he argues, will be savvier when electing its leaders. Taylor is a Pulitzer Prize-winning historian at the University of Virginia.

As you read, consider the following questions:

1. Why did the founders want the public to be educated?
2. Did the founders feel that the citizens needed to be educated about how to function in a democracy?
3. Why did the founders believe that the government should provide education to citizens?

Almost everyone praises education, but consensus dissolves over who should pay for it. This dilemma runs deep in our history, back to the founders who led the American Revolution and designed a more participatory form of government, known as a republic. They declared that Americans needed more and better education to preserve their state and national republics from relapsing into tyranny. A governor of Virginia, William H. Cabell, asserted in 1808 that education "constitutes one of the great pillars on which the civil liberties of a nation depend." More than a mere boon for individuals, education was a collective, social benefit essential for free government to endure.

Those founders worried that their 13 state republics, loosely tied in a new union, were vulnerable to internal divisions and external manipulation. They lived in a dangerous world dominated by empires and kingdoms run by monarchs and aristocrats who inherited and guarded their wealth and power. In European history, previous republics had been short-lived and usually small: cantons or city-states such as Pisa and Florence. How then could an immense and growing union of diverse states sustain a form of government that had always failed in the past? The American political experiments seemed especially threatened by contentions over balancing power between the states and the nation and between the regions: North and South, East and West. In addition to the North-South division that would nearly destroy the union during the 1860s, 18th-century Americans feared a violent split between the old states east of the Appalachians and the new settlements emerging in the vast watershed of the Mississippi River. Lacking a strong national identity, the people of 1787 identified with their states and distrusted outsiders. That pervasive distrust, rather than any common sense of nationalism, led the founders to craft the federal union as a "peace pact" meant to avert wars between the states.

American leaders worried that their imperial neighbors—French, Spanish, and especially British—would exploit the new nation's internal tensions to break up the tenuous union of the states. Poorly educated voters might also elect reckless demagogues who would appeal to class resentments and promote the violent redistribution of wealth. In such a nightmare scenario, a military despot—an American Caesar—ultimately would seize power and restore order at the expense of free government. John Adams warned the people, "When a favourable conjuncture has presented, some of the most intrigueing and powerful citizens have conceived the design of enslaving their country, and building their own greatness on its ruins. Philip and Alexander are examples of this in Greece—Caesar in Rome … and ten thousand others." Though a blessing for common people, a republic seemed dangerously fragile.

Republican political theory of the day held that empires and monarchies could thrive without an educated populace. Indeed, kings and nobles could better dominate and dazzle the ignorant and credulous. But republics depended on a broad electorate of common men, who, to keep their new rights, had to protect them with attentive care. These citizens, theorists insisted, needed to cultivate a special character known as "virtue": the precious capacity to transcend their diverse self-interests by favoring the common good of the political community. If everyone merely pursued his private interest, a republic would succumb to the perverse synergy of demagogues and tyrants. To override the selfishness assumed to be innately human, people had to be taught the value of virtue. Thomas Jefferson noted, "I have looked on our present state of liberty as a short-lived possession, unless the mass of the people could be informed to a certain degree."

To sustain their republics, American leaders felt compelled to reform the morals and manners of the nation's citizens. "We have changed our forms of government," Benjamin Rush declared, "but it remains yet to effect a revolution in our principles, opinions, and manners so as to accommodate them to the forms of government that we have adopted." Having grown up in colonies ruled by an empire committed to monarchy, the founders wanted the next generation of Americans to master a new culture of republicanism. Schools needed to produce well-informed protectors of republican government. "If the common people are ignorant and vicious," Rush concluded, "a republican nation can never be long free." A physician and reformer from Philadelphia, he sought to use education "to convert men into republican machines" in order to "fit them more easily for uniform and peaceable government." Putting revolutionary turmoil behind them, citizens had to become orderly supporters of the new state and federal governments. They also needed enough education to distinguish worthy from treacherous candidates for office—lest the republics succumb to those reckless demagogues or would-be aristocrats. As Jefferson put it, "Ignorance and despotism seem made for each other."

Reformers wanted more and better schools to endow young Americans with the cultural resources needed to protect the common good. During the colonial era, only New England's towns had sustained public grammar schools, and those towns mandated just a few weeks of schooling in the winter, when family farms needed less labor. Elsewhere in the new nation, the grammar schools were few and reliant on private tuition. Throughout the states, the children of wealthy families could learn Latin, advanced mathematics, and some science by going on to private academies. Colleges were even more expensive and exclusive. Neither women nor African Americans were permitted to attend, and few young white men could afford to. In 1800, the United States had only 18 colleges. The largest, Yale, had 217 students that year. Collectively, just 1,200 students attended college: fewer than one percent of adolescent males in the country.

Although home to many great revolutionary leaders, Virginia lacked any public schools and had but one small college—William & Mary, founded in 1693—and it was in financial decline. A third of adults could not read or write. Wealthy planters dominated the counties that constituted the new state. Loath to pay higher taxes to educate common whites, the gentry preferred to hire tutors to prepare their sons for private colleges in another state or in Britain. Jefferson regarded the county elites as self-perpetuating cabals of unworthy men, so he sought a more meritocratic and public educational system.

He distinguished between the old "artificial aristocracy" of inherited privilege and a new "natural aristocracy" of virtue and talents. Despite having inherited both wealth and slaves, Jefferson considered himself a natural rather than an artificial aristocrat because, he asserted, his commitment to serve common men proved his superior virtue. Through education, people could learn to think as active democrats, forsaking the passive deference that had elected old-style aristocrats to govern. "Worth and genius" should be, Jefferson preached, "sought out from every condition of life and compleately prepared by education for defeating the competition of wealth & birth for public trusts."

Jefferson wanted to weaken the old Virginia elite by broadening educational access for ordinary folk. He favored taxing the rich to educate the poor as essential for the common good. Jefferson assured George Washington, "It is an axiom in my mind that our liberty can never be safe but in the hands of the people themselves, and that too of the people with a certain degree of instruction. This it is the business of the state to effect, and on a general plan." Government had to act to reshape society. His friend and future president, James Monroe, agreed: "Being a high public concern, [education] ought to be provided for by the government itself."

In 1778, Jefferson proposed a radical educational system meant to transform Virginia along republican lines. To weaken the counties, he would subdivide them into several "hundreds," or townships, where through direct democracy the voters would build schools and hire teachers to educate every white girl and boy. The best boys (but no girls) would advance to county academies, where the rich would pay tuition but the best poor boy from each hundred school would earn a charity scholarship. In turn, the finest charity graduate from each academy would merit a college scholarship. With the bluntness of a natural aristocrat, Jefferson explained that, under his three-tiered system, "the best geniuses will be raked from the rubbish annually." His program had two goals, both political: to train for republican leadership "a few subjects in every state, to whom nature has given minds of the first order," and to enable every common man "to read, to judge & to vote understandingly on what is passing."

Radical for his time, if limited by our standards, Jefferson's proposal provided scant education for girls and none for African Americans, either free or enslaved. A practical politician, he knew that neither white voters nor leaders would spend a penny on educating blacks, who accounted for two-fifths of Virginia's people. Although Jefferson disliked slavery, he did not expend any political capital to challenge it in his home state, and he rebuffed a Quaker abolitionist who proposed to raise charitable funds to educate slaves. Jefferson warned that schooling could only deepen the unhappiness of the enslaved with their lot.

Despite his concessions to racial and gender inequality, Jefferson's system got nowhere in a revolutionary state at war with the British and already struggling to pay for military measures. Even the restoration of peace (in 1783) and of prosperity (after 1790) did not endear educational reform to Virginia's legislators. In 1796, they belatedly passed a watered-down bill that invited county governments to put in place Jefferson's system but left it to them to raise the taxes to finance it. Only one of Virginia's more than 100 counties implemented even part of the system during the next 20 years. County leaders balked at taxing themselves to educate the poor. In vain, Jefferson argued that "the tax which will be paid for this purpose is not more than the thousandth part of what will be paid to kings, priests, and nobles who will rise up among us if we leave the people in ignorance."

The failure of Jefferson's proposal distressed the small pool of well-educated Virginians. In 1804, William Wirt, later the attorney general of the United States, praised the "astonishing greatness" of the plan to rescue genius from "obscurity, indigence, and ignorance" while giving "stability and solid glory to the republic!" Wirt worried that Virginia lacked "the animating soul of a republic. I mean, public spirit. ... There seems to me to be but one object throughout the state: to grow rich." In 1809, the state's governor, John Tyler (the father of the future president), rebuked the legislators: "There cannot be a subject of more importance, in a free government ... and yet so fatal is that apathy which prevails, or so parsimonious a policy has insinuated itself among us, that year after year is permitted to pass away without a single attempt to attain so great and so indispensable an object." As a result, Tyler traveled about the state and reported, "Scarcely a common country school is to be found capable of teaching the mother tongue grammatically."

Jefferson was half-right to blame county oligarchs, but it was state legislators who had passed the buck to the counties rather than raise state taxes to fund public education. And those legislators answered to voters who also did not like paying taxes. David Watson, a friend of Jefferson's, supported public education as a member of the Virginia General Assembly, but he lost his bid for reelection. Watson blamed common voters for "being so ignorant as they are, that our gentlemen are not more anxious to get learning and knowledge." In a satirical essay, Watson insisted that common Virginians preferred to buy new boots for their sons, peach brandy for themselves, and bonnets for their wives rather than fund education. He doubted that there was "sense enough among the great bulk of the people to prevent a few cunning, ambitious men from taking our houses and land and every thing else away from us; and then how shall we get boots, bonnets and brandy?"

Governor Tyler agreed: "He who can go back from the assembly and tell his constituents he has saved a penny secures his popularity against the next Election." Tyler expressed this lament in a confidential letter to Jefferson, likening the public to a patient in denial: "It is sometimes necessary to conceal the healing medicine from the patient, lest his sickly appetite may reject that which alone can bring him health and life."

Here then was the rub. Visionary leaders insisted that preserving a republic required improving the common people by an increased investment in education. But a republic depended on common voters who lacked schooling and often balked at paying for it, preferring to spend their money on consumer goods. As farmers, they also wanted to keep their children at work on the farm. To justify their preferences, they invoked a populist distrust of the educated. A rustic republican from North Carolina insisted, "College learned persons give themselves great airs, are proud, and the fewer of them we have amongst us the better." Preferring "the plain, simple, honest matter-of-fact republicanism," he asked, "Who wants Latin and Greek and abstruse mathematics at these times and in a country like this?" Distrustful of all aristocrats, natural and artificial, he insisted that they should pay to educate themselves, and the poor could make do without book learning; thus, he would vote for candidates who kept taxes low. Common voters in the southern states often did not regard education as essential to preserving their republic.

In old age, after retiring as president of the United States, Jefferson sought to revive at least half of his educational program in Virginia. During the late 1810s, the state expected a windfall in federal money to reimburse Virginia for damages and expenditures during the recently concluded War of 1812. The state also reaped new funds by chartering bank and canal corporations. The enhanced revenue sufficed to fund a new state university or a broad system of local, public schools for common people—but not both. Jefferson and his legislative allies favored a university and located it in his hometown of Charlottesville, sucking up almost all of the state's available funds for education. He reasoned that the new university would train a natural aristocracy for Virginia, and during the next generation, the graduates would (he hoped) belatedly create the public system of common schools. His wishful thinking faltered, for the new university educated the sons of wealth and privilege, who perpetuated those advantages when they became the state's legislators and governors. By compromising his full vision for education, Jefferson unwittingly delayed the creation of educational opportunity for most Virginians for half a century.

A different model of reform emerged in the northern states, where slavery was vanishing and society sustained a larger middle class. In the North, the educational reformers included Jedediah Peck of Otsego County in upstate New York. During the 1790s, Peck was a self-educated farmer, carpenter, and preacher among fellow settlers who had migrated from New England. Ambitious and resourceful, he won a seat in the state legislature by expressing the resentments and aspirations of his common neighbors, who felt insulted by the condescension of the wealthy lawyers and landlords who ran the county and state governments. Peck promoted social mobility and equality by demanding state funding for a new system of public education. He wanted to "bring improvement within the reach and power of the humblest citizen" because, Peck emphasized, true liberty required educated citizens: "In all countries where education is confined to a few people, we always find arbitrary governments and abject slavery."

In the legislature, he kept pushing for appropriations for common country schools, and in 1812, New York became the first state outside New England to adopt a comprehensive system for educating all children in grammar schools. Such public systems gradually spread throughout the middle-Atlantic and midwestern states during the 1820s and 1830s but not in the South, which had none until after the Civil War. The conviction that freedom required education flourished only where slavery had been disavowed. Northerners paid for the expansion of educational opportunity with their tax dollars because they anticipated economic benefits.

The growth of colleges and universities followed, accelerating over the generations, particularly in the North. By 1840, about 16,000 Americans attended 173 colleges, most of them small and religiously oriented. Forty years later, the United States had more than 85,000 students in 591 institutions of higher learning, which included some new, larger, and secular state universities. The percentage of young adults attending college had doubled from 1800 but still accounted for just two percent of the people in that age group. The 20th century brought the greatest leap forward, from four percent of young adults in 1900 to nearly 50 percent by 1980. (The United States now leads the world in the proportion of college graduates.) The growth reflected an economic transformation as most Americans moved away from agriculture into industry, government bureaucracies, or commercial services. Corporate managers, professionals, and bureaucrats needed the training and certification of a college education to land and keep a good job. Until the 1970s, voters supported increased investment in education as a political priority.

In the process of that expansion, education gradually became redefined as an economic good, rather than a political one. The proponents of higher education promised economic growth, not political virtue, as the prime goal. It became quaint at best to raise an alarm about demagogues and aristocrats as the dangerous consequence of an ignorant electorate. Many students valued economic and social mobility over the responsibilities of civic leadership. And only a political fool would seek virtue in an electorate bombarded by advertising that urged Americans to keep score of winners and losers by the consumer goods that they could buy and display. Today, we have more boots, bonnets, and brandy than ever before and are now expected to pursue our self-interest as voters much as we do as consumers.

The shift to an economic justification for education has led to its redefinition as a private, individual benefit instead of a public good. In the wake of the Second World War, the GI Bill funded students on a vast scale, allowing them to pursue any major, including those that did not lead immediately to a particular job, enabling them to exercise a choice denied to current students by the financial exigencies of high costs and mounting debts. Today, we justify that constraint on their choices by assuming that the individual student is the primary beneficiary of education and that its value is best measured in dollars subsequently earned.

"A typical college graduate can expect to make over half a million dollars more than a nongraduate over a lifetime," Quoctrung Bui recently wrote in *The New York Times*. Indeed, it now sounds fuzzy and naïve to speak of any other benefits of higher education, such as knowledge for its own sake, increased happiness, an enhanced appreciation of art, or a deeper understanding of human nature and society. Along the way, we also have shunted into the background the collective, social rewards of education: the ways in which we all, including those who do not attend college, benefit from better writers and thinkers, technological advances, expanded markets, and lower crime rates. Above all, we need to return to Jefferson's emphasis on rational inquiry built on evidence—or risk the republic's fate on politicians who appeal to our emotions and prejudices.

Those prejudices have led to a comparable assault on public funding for K–12 schools, ominously rebranded "government schools" by critics who seek to discredit them. These critics associate public education with a demonized concept of all government, even state and local, as undemocratic. In the process, legislators disproportionately reduce funding for schools in the poorest districts with the greatest numbers of immigrants and people of color. Taking the lead in this assault, the Kansas legislature and Governor Sam Brownback provoked the state's supreme court to denounce the state's draconian new funding formula for creating "intolerable, and simply unfair, wealth-based disparities among the districts."

We have come to think and speak of education as primarily economic (rather than political) and individual (rather than social) in its rewards. As a consequence, growing numbers of voters care only for the education of their own children. These conceptual and rhetorical shifts lead legislators to wonder why taxpayers should pay for the education of others—particularly those of poorer means, different culture, or darker color. If only the individual, rather than society as a whole, benefits from education, let the student bear the cost of it: so runs the new reasoning.

During every recession, state governments make budget cuts, and public colleges and universities become the tempting, soft targets. That temptation grows when states feel pinched by rising costs for Medicaid and prisons (places stuffed with the poorly educated). By reducing public support for colleges and universities, legislators and governors induce them to increase the tuition and fees that students pay. A recent report by the Center on Budget and Policy Priorities finds that since the 2008 recession, states have reduced spending on public higher education by 17 percent per student. During the same period, tuition has risen by 33 percent. The University of California system is the largest in the nation. According to the American Academy of Arts and Sciences, the state of California provided a quarter of the system's budget in 2002. After a billion dollars in cuts, the state now pays for just nine percent of the system's costs, yet legislators howl in outrage when university administrators admit more out-of-state and foreign students, who can be charged twice as much as in-state students. The same game is playing out in every state.

Increasingly reliant on loans to cover the cost of higher education, students have assumed alarming levels of debt: an estimated $1.3 trillion owed by 42 million Americans. According to the August issue of *Consumer Reports,* graduates this year average $37,000 in debt per student. The debt burden puts a drag on the overall economy and society, as thousands of graduates delay buying a home or having children. Increasingly, young people from middle-class families question whether attending college is worth the cost.

As a country, we are in retreat from the Jefferson and Peck dream of equal educational opportunity for all. And the future social costs will be high. Proportionally fewer Americans will benefit from higher education, inequality will increase, and free government will become a stage set for opportunists to pander to the prejudices and fears of the poorly educated.

Although the current definition of education is relentlessly economic, the source of the crisis is political. Just as in Jefferson's day, most legislators and governors believe that voters prefer tax cuts to investments in public education. Too few leaders make the case for higher education as a public good from which everyone benefits. But broader access to a quality education pays off in collective ways: economic growth, scientific innovation, informed voters and leaders, a richer and more diverse culture, and lower crime rates—each of which benefits us all. Few Americans know the political case for education advanced by the founders. Modern politicians often make a great show of their supposed devotion to those who founded the nation, but then push for the privatization of education as just another consumer product best measured in dollars and paid for by individuals. This reverses the priorities of the founders.

Americans lost something valuable when we forsook "virtue" as a goal for education and a foundation for free government. In 1950, a Harvard committee published an influential report titled *General Education in a Free Society*. The authors wrote that "our society, like any society, rests on common beliefs and … a major task of education is to perpetuate them." But the report struggled to define the "common beliefs" best taught by modern American universities. In the 19th century, most colleges had promoted a patriotism linked to Protestant Christianity. But in our own century, no one creed seems capable of encompassing the diverse backgrounds and values of American students. We also balk at empowering any public institution to teach a particular political orthodoxy. The sole common ground is a celebration of the university as a "marketplace of ideas," where every individual can pick and choose her or his values. Secular universities preach just one core value: the open and free investigation of multiple ideas. Liberal education now favors a process of free choice rather than any other particular belief.

We need to revive the founders' definition of education as a public good and an essential pillar of free government. We should also recover their concept of virtue, classically defined, as a core public value worth teaching. That, in turn, would enable more voters to detect demagogues seeking power through bluster and bombast and pandering to the self-interest of members of the electorate. At the end of the Constitutional Convention of 1787, a woman in Philadelphia is said to have asked Benjamin Franklin what sort of government the delegates had created for the people. He supposedly replied, "A republic, madam, if you can keep it."

Viewpoint 4

> *"The People and the intelligentsia are at war, and it wasn't The People who started it. "*

Populism May Not Be What You Think It Is

John Emerson

In the following viewpoint, written three years before Donald Trump won the US presidency on a wave of political energy that many have described as populism, John Emerson takes up the question of what is populism. He gives a short history of the phenomenon and explains how the meaning and use of the term has changed over the years. The lesson then moves to events of today, when Emerson argues that, thanks to the influence of big money on both parties, the United States is moving back into a situation when the average person is not represented. This, he says, leads to populism. Emerson lives in Portland, Oregon.

As you read, consider the following questions:

1. Why, according to this author, is "populism" so difficult to define?
2. How does Emerson think that populist have been misunderstood and misrepresented recently?
3. How has the Democratic party moved away from representing the average American?

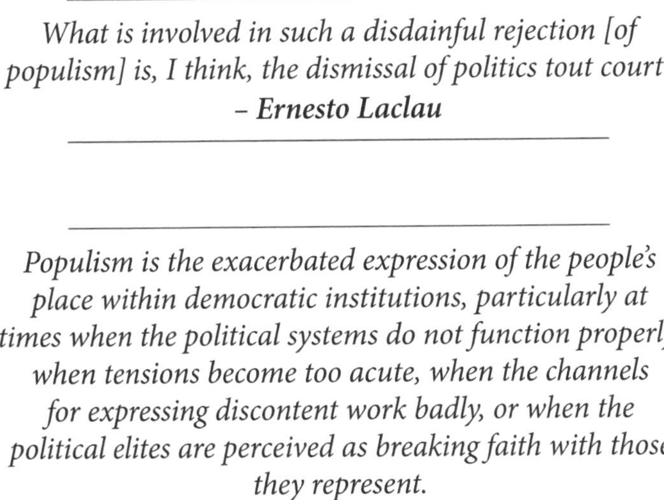

What is involved in such a disdainful rejection [of populism] is, I think, the dismissal of politics tout court.
– Ernesto Laclau

Populism is the exacerbated expression of the people's place within democratic institutions, particularly at times when the political systems do not function properly, when tensions become too acute, when the channels for expressing discontent work badly, or when the political elites are perceived as breaking faith with those they represent.
– Meny and Surel

Everyone is talking about populism, but no one can define it." The opening sentence of Gellner's introduction to the 1971 anthology Populism: Its National Characteristics remains more or less true today—in Laclau's words, "A persistent feature of the literature on populism is its reluctance—or difficulty—in giving the concept any precise meaning". As a result, anyone can be a populist. Rush Limbaugh drinks $300 bottles of wine and vacations in the south of France, and he's a populist. The Koch brothers are two of the ten richest Americans, and they're populists. Rand Paul is a goldbug, and he's a populist. The requirements are easy to meet: you just have to be angry, anti-intellectual, bigoted, demagogic, and right wing. (You know who else was a populist? Hitler.) And as I've found, all good liberals, Democrats, radicals, and political scientists steer clear of populism.

The received definition (or non-definition) of Populism does not square with what I know about the American Populists, American Populist-like movements and political leaders since that time, or American political history in general, and in my opinion it has had a severely negative effect on American politics and on the Democratic Party since 1948 or so. So I will begin by writing not about the history of Populism, or the history of populism, but the history of the term "populism".

As common nouns the words "populism" and "populist" came into use rather late, almost always in a polemical context, and social science's appropriation of this weakly-defined term (generalized from several very dissimilar political movements) was also tendentious and polemical. "Populism", whatever else it may or not be, is the unthought Other of social science and of the administrative politics dominant in much of the developed world. Most definitions of populism hold that populists define themselves in opposition to the elitist Other, but since elitists also define their work in opposition to the populist's folk understanding of their lives, it's a chicken-and-egg problem.

II.

The 1920 Oxford English Dictionary and the 1988 Webster's Unabridged take "populism" and "populist" to refer specifically to the American Populist Party of the 1890s (and the slightly-earlier Russian Narodniks). These two groups were similar mostly in name: the Narodniks were revolutionary socialist urban intellectuals who tried unsuccessfully to instigate a peasant uprising, whereas the American Populists were farmers and countryfolk (but not peasants) who worked within the electoral system and merely asked for adjustments to the capitalist system, albeit rather large ones. (The German word Volkisch also can be translated "populist," but this does not mean, for example, that the American: populists were Volkisch in the continental sense).

To my knowledge the first uses of the term "populist" in the generic sense (rather than as a word designating the historical Populists and Narodniks) came in 1934-5 in two articles in the New York Times used the term to describe Father Coughlin, Huey Long, and Upton Sinclair (who was actually a Socialist). The generic use of the term finally appeared in the Second Edition of the OED, citing a highly-pejorative 1958 reference by Walter Laqueur highlighting populist antisemitism—as well as a rather more sympathetic 1969 use of the term in the book Student Power edited by one Alexander Cockburn.

The generic term made its entry into social science after World War Two, and the classical definitions of the term are to be found in Hofstadter's The Age of Reform (1955) and Gellner and Ionescu's Populism: Its National Characteristics (1969), which includes a contribution from Hofstadter. Hofstadter's revisionist portrait of the Populists has itself required massive revision, but this interpretation is still canonical in political science and within the Democratic Party. Gellner's anthology, which tries to generalize the term historically and geographically, has had a comparable influence at the higher academic levels, and by now populism is defined primarily in terms of nationalism, sexism, bigotry, and anti-intellectualism—albeit usually with a pro forma concession that populists often do express real grievances of real people. Supposedly populist national leaders included Peron, Vargas, Sukarno, Nkrumah (and perhaps even Castro!) in the third world, all of them anti-American, and European populists included Poujade, Haider, and many others. As the debate proceeded, particularly when Europe was in question, Vienna's late 19th century mayor Karl Lueger came to be taken as another prototypical populist: Lueger did many good things, but was also an antisemite much admired by Hitler. (The "politics of the stammtisch"—or pub—mentioned by Mudde was Lueger's specialty). This is a very big tent, as many have noted: Narodniks, American Populists, proto-Nazis, third world national leaders, and European malcontents were all lumped together. Populists can be working class or middle class, urban or rural, conservative or radical, militarist or isolationist, pious or secular, left or right, national or local, and almost anything else. It's like pornography: "I can't define it, but I know it when I see it".

III.

The post-WWII debate about populism took place during an embattled period of transition. America's anti-fascist war liberalism was being replaced by anti-Communist war liberalism, and many people had to purge their resumes or be purged themselves. In the aftermath of Hitler and under the shadow of Stalin, many radicals and liberals inclined to pessimism, in particular pessimism about majoritarian politics, while positively working to develop an anti-majoritarian, elitist form of Democratic liberalism on the model of technocratic war liberalism and urban machine politics. The intellectual founders of this new politics were mostly social scientists, and many of them were tempted by the siren of value-free anti-ideology and flew that flag, but at the distance of half a century they can clearly be seen to be engagé ideologues. Important figures included Daniel Bell, Edward Shils, Seymour Martin Lipset, Arthur Schlesinger, John Kenneth Galbraith, Chester Bowles, Reinhold Niebuhr, Richard Hofstadter, and Walter Lippmann (the father of them all, and also the father of the neoliberal Mont Pelerin Society). Some of these men had ties with the "New York Intellectuals" and with such emigres as Hannah Arendt and Theodor Adorno and (more distantly) Hayek, von Mises, Leo Strauss, and their coteries. Hofstadter was the American history expert of the group and was most responsible for the negative view of the Populists and the pejorative definition of "populism" which have been dominant (in a rather simplified and dogmatic forms less nuanced than Hofstadter's) in the Democratic Party and the American intelligentsia since then.

The embattled context colored Hofstadter's writing. To Hofstadter, populism was Joe McCarthy destroying the careers of people like himself. Populism was Hitler. Populism was lynch mobs. Populism was the Union Party running against Roosevelt in 1936, and the progressives who withdrew support from Roosevelt after Roosevelt's 1937 austerity budget and the court-packing plan. Populism was the isolationists who failed to support American involvement in WWII, even though Hofstadter himself had dabbled in isolationism. Populism was the Progressive Party refusing to support Truman. Hofstadter's populism wasn't really about the Populist Party, much less the Narodniks, but about the terrible Crowd, Mob, or Mass which was feared both by conservative and by liberal theorists of the time (and which was blamed for Hitler)

Hofstadter adored Adlai Stevenson, above all when Stevenson described himself as a conservative, and Hofstadter's political dream was an elitist, semi-technocratic anti-majoritarian party led by intellectuals on the model of what he thought the "wet" British Conservative party to be—a gentlemanly party without agitators, dissidents, and other such inconveniences. And by and large, some version of his view became canonical, both in the intellectual world and in the Democratic Party.

After the 1948 election the Democrats no longer fought big business: "Liberals are not afraid of bigness" and "A rising tide lifts all boats" were the slogans. Rather than supporting labor, the Democrats mediated between their labor friends and their corporate friends, and when necessary they busted the unions. All opposition to military adventures was rejected by the Democrats as isolationist or pinko. The Democrats had already conducted their own purge of the American sympathizers of America's former Eastasian ally when McCarthy came along, and while not all Democrats supported Joe McCarthy the way the Kennedys did, Democratic opposition was feeble and late. In many respects the neocons and the neoliberals were already there in 1948.

IV.

After 1948 or thereabouts populism has primarily been defined as "anti-elitism"—often simply as a demagogic political style or as an inarticulate political mood. However, both the Narodniks and the American Populists defined themselves in terms of class and power and had concrete political goals, not just opposition to a sinister elite, and despite some of the rhetoric of these two groups, I doubt that the contemporary definition of "populism" applies to them at all. The concocted "populist" label, an artifact of post-

WWII politics, was applied backwards in history by Hofstadter and others, to serve as the underpinning for their justification of the antipopular postwar, post-New-Deal Democratic party as it had developed between 1937 and 1948; and after that it was easy enough to fit in various European and international groups not in conformity with the postwar brand of liberalism/socialism.

The postwar transformation of the Democratic Party was part and parcel of the technocratic transformation both of government and the university, and a concommitant development was a technocratic-academic-cultural voting demographic. During WWII the university's role mushroomed – even literary critics and anthropologists were able to get on the gravy train. All during the 20th century the political role of the university had been increasing, and even though the New Deal was driven politically to a considerable degree by populist / radical pressure, and (along with the urban machines and the white supremacist bosses) Roosevelt relied heavily on his technocratic brain trust. Coming out of the war, the US had a new political-managerial-scientific-academic elite—both an integral part of the government and a voting demographic.

Hofstadter and his friends belonged to this elite, and "populism" was its most feared enemy. The various, often mutually-incompatible definitions of populism, and the disparate examples scavenged from history, all are intelligible once you ask who the enemies of the "populists" were. Populists are the Other of the liberal / left intelligentsia, and all populists are guilty of all of the crimes of any populist. (Leninists are as anti-populist as liberals, and Hofstadter , an ex-pinko, was able to retrofit many of the Communist anti-populist slurs for liberal use).

Or to put it in more contemporary terms, populists are the Other of the dominated fraction of the dominant class: the intellectuals and the political-managerial-scientific-academic elite. Populists are the less-educated mass of the poor and middling (lower middle) classes—the people without taste, class, and style —or more simply, the majority. Even today a certain proportion of the intelligentsia have plebian backgrounds (though this is less true by the year). Anyone who has made the jump can remember the hazing period at the start of introductory classes, when the student finds out that everything that he knows (and everything anyone in his reference group knows) is wrong. To be admitted into the elite, you have to believe three impossible things before breakfast, and those who fail to do this are squeezed out, usually in an especially humiliating fashion. In PolSci 101 you learn that "By the people, for the people, and of the people" is pure disastrous nonsense. The "counterfactual assumptions" of Econ 101 are too many to count, but since there's a lot of money in econ, Students eagerly play along. Examples can be multiplied from other disciplines.

Distancing the student from his own experience and from his origins is not incidental to education, but one education's main purposes. Bourdieu speaks of expressing the "particular existence" in a "misrecognizable form" at an "objective [neutralizing] distance from necessity and from those trapped within it". Academic "political 'alienation'....like the aesthetic 'alienation', can neutralize the immediate presence, the urgency and the functions of the object." Even secondary schooling "by at least slightly initiating its pupils into legitimate culture and its values, introduces a break with the popular world view." (Distinction, pp. 54, 55, 446, 447).

So The People and the intelligentsia are at war, and it wasn't The People who started it. When Hofstadter cites the Jacksonian Davy Crockett ("This college system went into practice to draw a line of demarcation between the two classes of society – it separated the children of the rich from the children of the poor") he almost could be citing Bourdieu.

V.

I got interested in Populism / populism around 2002 when I found out how aggressively anti-populist many Democrats were—both party pros and the more educated rank and file. I started reading the literature on populism and the Populists and came to feel that the Populists had been misrepresented. Up until that point I had taken some degree of populism as being a defining trait of the Democratic Party, but as I found out, this is hardly true at all except opportunistically during campaigns (and, I may say, locally in Minnesota). Meanwhile, Republican populism was all over the place—someone who only watched TV might end up thinking that the typical Republican was a construction worker, cowboy, or plumber. I summed up the initial phase of my investigation with the phrase "Republican populism is fake, but democratic elitism is real", and I still think that this characterization is accurate.

The anti-populism of the Democratic machine is not mysterious: the Democratic Party has chosen to rely on media-heavy campaigns requiring massive fundraising from plutocrats in finance, Hollywood, and elsewhere. (Needless to say, the Democratic pros get a tasty cut of this fundraising). I ended up concluding that this was not recent, however, and that the roots of neoliberal, neocon, "centrist" Democratic Party go all the way back to the 1940s, and furthermore, that a major Democratic voting demographic was, in fact, highly educated elitists. (Almost 10% of the American electorate has a postgraduate degree, most of them Democrats).

My concern is not for the future of the Democratic Party. It's quite possible that the present pluralist, neoliberal, neocon alliance of big money, the educated elite, and the various sorts of minorities might be victorious in the future, especially if the Tea Party succeeds in destructing the Republican Party. My concern is with the consequences of the continued domination of big money and antipopular ideology. We are very close to the situation in 1890 and before, when two plutocratic parties fought out elections on the basis of cultural differences which were politically rather irrelevant – Northern Protestants and Southern blacks vs. Southern whites and Northern ethnics). During this period the average American, especially in the West, had no representation, and that's where Populism came from. And that's where we are today.

As might be guessed, I favor a more populist Democratic Party, and a return to the "us against them" / "poor against rich" political strategy. Whether this is possible I do not know. A big chunk of the Democratic Party would just as soon be socially-liberal Republicans, if such a thing were possible, and these Democrats are horrified by the possibility of white trash populism (as they see it). At the same time, a big chunk of the target "poor" demographic (though not as big a chunk as people think) has been recruited into conservative bigotry, and an even bigger chunk is apolitical and demoralized; and a big chunk of the not-yet-poor seem to have decided to ride things out while everyone else gets screwed —neoliberalism is good at backloading problems and putting the pain into the future. (But no, the Tea Party is not made up of the white trash poor. They tend to be middle class and even educated).

Whether anyone knows it or not, since 2008 we have been in the longest and deepest recession (in terms of unemployment) since 1937, and tens of millions have lost their homes and/or their retirement savings. The major players are using these present problems as a pretext for the restructuring the American class system on the 19th century model, with an uneducated, disenfranchised, servile, impoverished working class. This should be a time for pitchforks, but the political response has been feeble. The Democratic Party in its present antipopular form, and any left party as antipopular as most leftists seem to be, could hardly respond effectively to a crisis of this type.

And indeed, they haven't.

Viewpoint 5

> *"It is clear that citizens today express less of an attachment to liberal democracy."*

Democracy in the West Is Not as Robust as Most People Believe

Roberto Stefan Foa and Yascha Mounk

In the following viewpoint, Roberto Stefan Foa and Yascha Mounk examine the signs and indications that Democracy in the West is undergoing deconsolidation—that is, becoming more fragile. The authors cite data indicating that much of the trend toward deconsolidation has already begun in the West. However, they offer some hope for what can be done to make democracy more robust. Foa is a lecturer in Political Science at the University of Australia in Melbourne. Mounk is a lecturer in Political Theory at Harvard University in Cambridge, Massachusetts.

As you read, consider the following questions:

1. What data do the authors use to make their case that democracy in the West is weakening?
2. What is a "cohort" effect?
3. Why might young people in particular be willing to abandon Democracy?

For four decades, *Die Welt*, one of West Germany's leading newspapers, refused to acknowledge the existence of an East German state. Since the paper's editors expected the communist regime to collapse within a matter of years, they put scare quotes around its initials whenever they discussed the German Democratic Republic (GDR). While other papers reported about the policies pursued by the GDR, *Die Welt* unfailingly wrote about the "GDR."

Sometime in the summer of 1989, the paper's leadership finally decided to give up on the pretense that the East German regime was on the verge of collapse. The communists had been in power for so long, and seemed so well-entrenched, that the scare quotes had become an embarrassing denial of reality. On 2 August 1989, reporters were allowed to drop the scare quotes when writing about the GDR for the first time in the paper's history. Three months later, the Berlin Wall fell. On 3 October 1990, the GDR ceased to exist.

The editors of *Die Welt* radically misjudged the signs of the times. At precisely the moment when they should have realized that support for the communist regime was dwindling, they finally reconciled themselves to its durability. They were hardly alone. The collective failure of social scientists, policy makers, and journalists to take seriously the possibility that the Soviet bloc might collapse should serve as a warning. Even the best-trained and most methodologically rigorous scholars are liable to assume that the recent past is a reliable guide to the future, and that extreme events are not going to happen.

Three decades ago, most scholars simply assumed that the Soviet Union would remain stable. This assumption was suddenly proven false. Today, we have even greater confidence in the durability of the world's affluent, consolidated democracies. But do we have good grounds for our democratic self-confidence? At first sight, there would seem to be some reason for concern. Over the last three decades, trust in political institutions such as parliaments or the courts has precipitously declined across the established democracies of North America and Western Europe. So has voter turnout. As party identification has weakened and party membership has declined, citizens have become less willing to stick with establishment parties. Instead, voters increasingly endorse single-issue movements, vote for populist candidates, or support "antisystem" parties that define themselves in opposition to the status quo. Even in some of the richest and most politically stable regions of the world, it seems as though democracy is in a state of serious disrepair.

Most political scientists, however, have steadfastly declined to view these trends as an indication of structural problems in the functioning of liberal democracy, much less as a threat to its very existence. A wide range of leading scholars, including Ronald Inglehart, Pippa Norris, Christian Welzel, and Russell J. Dalton, have generally interpreted these trends as benign indications of the increasing political sophistication of younger generations of "critical" citizens who are less willing to defer to traditional elites. Keeping with a distinction made by David Easton in 1975, many scholars acknowledge that "government legitimacy," or support for particular governments, has declined. But they also insist that "regime legitimacy," or support for democracy as a system of government, remains robust. Thus people may increasingly feel that democracy is not working well in their country or that the government of the day is doing a poor job, but this only makes them all the more appreciative of the fact that liberal democracy allows them to protest the government or vote it out of office. According to this view, democracies such as France, Sweden, and the United States remain as consolidated and stable today as they ever have been.

In our view, however, this optimistic interpretation may no longer be tenable. Drawing on data from Waves 3 through 6 of the World Values Surveys (1995–2014), we look at four important types of measures that are clear indicators of regime legitimacy as opposed to government legitimacy: citizens' express support for the system as a whole; the degree to which they support key institutions of liberal democracy, such as civil rights; their willingness to advance their political causes within the existing political system; and their openness to authoritarian alternatives such as military rule.

What we find is deeply concerning. Citizens in a number of supposedly consolidated democracies in North America and Western Europe have not only grown more critical of their political leaders. Rather, they have also become more cynical about the value of democracy as a political system, less hopeful that anything they do might influence public policy, and more willing to express support for authoritarian alternatives. The crisis of democratic legitimacy extends across a much wider set of indicators than previously appreciated.

How much importance do citizens of developed countries ascribe to living in a democracy? Among older generations, the devotion to democracy is about as fervent and widespread as one might expect: In the United States, for example, people born during the interwar period consider democratic governance an almost sacred value. When asked to rate on a scale of 1 to 10 how "essential" it is for them "to live in a democracy," 72 percent of those born before World War II check "10," the highest value. So do 55 percent of the same cohort in the Netherlands. But, shows, the millennial generation (those born since 1980) has grown much more indifferent. Only one in three Dutch millennials accords maximal importance to living in a democracy; in the United States, that number is slightly lower, around 30 percent.[1]

The decline in support for democracy is not just a story of the young being more critical than the old; it is, in the language of survey research, owed to a "cohort" effect rather than an "age" effect. Back in 1995, for example, only 16 percent of Americans born in the 1970s (then in their late teens or early twenties) believed that democracy was a "bad" political system for their country. Twenty years later, the number of "antidemocrats" in this same generational cohort had increased by around 4 percentage points, to 20 percent. The next cohort—comprising those born in the 1980s—is even more antidemocratic: In 2011, 24 percent of U.S. millennials (then in their late teens or early twenties) considered democracy to be a "bad" or "very bad" way of running the country. Although this trend was somewhat more moderate in Europe, it was nonetheless significant: In 2011, 13 percent of European youth (aged 16 to 24) expressed such a view, up from 8 percent among the same age group in the mid-1990s.

Public-opinion data thus suggest a significant generational reversal. Not so long ago, young people were much more enthusiastic than older people about democratic values: In the first waves of the World Values Survey, in 1981–84 and 1990–93, young respondents were much keener than their elders on protecting freedom of speech and significantly less likely to embrace political radicalism. Today, the roles have reversed: On the whole, support for political radicalism in North America and Western Europe is higher among the young, and support for freedom of speech lower.[2]

Withdrawal from Democratic Institutions

People can have an abstract allegiance to "democracy" while simultaneously rejecting many key norms and institutions that have traditionally been regarded as necessary ingredients of democratic governance. Therefore, if we are to understand why levels of support for democracy have changed, we must study the ways in which people's conception of democracy, as well as their degree of engagement with democratic institutions, have changed.[3] Beyond support for regular elections, which are essential even according to the most minimal interpretation of democracy, full-fledged support for democracy should also entail a commitment to liberal values such as the protection of key rights and civil liberties, as well as a willingness to use the institutions of liberal democracy to effect political change.[4] So how have political participation and support for liberal democracy fared in the recent past?

A battery of questions on interpretations of democracy was not fielded in the World Values Survey until 2005, so there is not enough time-series data to measure directly how citizens' understanding of democracy has evolved over time. It is possible, however, to analyze differences between generational cohorts as a proxy. Taking the pooled data from Europe and the United States, we find that attitudes toward liberal institutions do not differ radically among different generations. But a liberal conception of democracy is somewhat less entrenched among millennials (born since the 1980s) than their baby-boomer parents (born during the first two decades after the Second World War). In the United States, for example, 41 percent of those born during the interwar and initial postwar decades state that it is "absolutely essential" in a democracy that "civil rights protect people's liberty." Among millennials, this share falls to 32 percent. In the European Union, these figures are 45 and 39 percent, respectively.

Any minimally liberal understanding of representative democracy needs to encompass the notion that elections should be free and fair. So it is disquieting that in mature democracies such an interpretation of democracy, though still endorsed by a clear majority of the population, is weaker among younger voters. In the United States, for example, only 10 percent of citizens born in the interwar years and 14 percent of baby-boomers say that it is "unimportant" in a democracy for people to "choose their leaders in free elections" (with "unimportant" defined as 1 to 5 on a 10-point scale of importance). Among millennials, this figure rises to 26 percent. In Europe, there is a similar, though less dramatic, pattern, with 9 percent of the interwar and baby-boomer generations versus 13 percent of millennials responding that free and fair elections are unimportant. (Since we lack time-series data on these measures, these findings are preliminary and will have to be confirmed by future surveys.) Moreover, there is no broad reason to assume that young people should, in general, be prone to a less liberal interpretation of democracy, as the opposite pattern is found in places such as China, India, and sub-Saharan Africa.

The health of a democracy depends not only on support for key political values such as civil rights, but also on the active participation of an informed citizenry. Indeed, following in the tradition of Gabriel Almond and Sidney Verba's classic 1963 work *The Civic Culture*, successive studies have shown that civic engagement affects democracy's ability to deliver public goods, to hold officials accountable, and to provide effective government. This makes it all the more troubling that there has been a long-documented withdrawal from formal democratic participation: Since the 1960s, voter turnout has fallen and political-party membership has plummeted in virtually all established democracies.

Just as younger generations are less committed to the importance of democracy, so too are they less likely to be politically engaged. In fact, in both Western Europe and North America, interest in politics has rapidly and markedly declined among the young. At the same time, it has either remained stable or even increased among older cohorts. As a result, overall levels of engagement have remained steady at around 60 percent in the United States and about 50 percent in Europe. In other words, the aggregate figure, important as it is in its own right, masks the most striking part of the story: the quickly widening generational gap in political apathy.

In 1990, both a majority of young Americans (those between the ages of 16 and 35) and a majority of older Americans (36 years and older) reported being "fairly interested" or "very interested" in politics—53 and 63 percent, respectively. By 2010, the share of young Americans professing an interest in politics had dropped by more than 12 percentage points and the share of older Americans had risen by 4 percentage points. As a result, the generation gap had widened from 10 percentage points to 26 percentage points. Among European respondents, who on the whole report less interest in politics than do their American counterparts, this phenomenon is even starker: The gap between young and old more than tripled between 1990 and 2010, from 4 to 14 percentage points. This is attributable almost solely to a rapid loss of interest among young respondents. Whereas the share of Europeans aged 36 or older who were interested in politics remained stable at 52 percent, among the young that figured dropped from 48 to 38 percent.

In both advanced and emerging democracies, the generation that came of age during the 1960s withdrew from traditional forms of political engagement, such as joining political parties and voting. This trend has continued, with millennials even less likely than their parents to participate in the democratic system via formal institutions. Most scholars have resisted the conclusion that young people are worryingly disengaged from democratic politics by arguing that a decline in conventional forms of political participation has been compensated for by a rise in "nonconventional" forms of activism, such as membership in new social movements or participation in protests and boycotts.[5] Recent data from Wave 5 (2005–2009) and Wave 6 (2010–14) of the World Values Survey, however, suggest that this no longer holds true: The baby-boomer generation has not managed to transfer its proclivity to engage in non- conventional forms of activism to its children and grandchildren. As a result, more recent generations are not just disengaged from the formal institutions of liberal democracy; they are also less likely to participate in nonconventional political activities, such as joining new social movements or participating in political protest.

Historically, citizens have been more likely to engage in protests when they are young. So it is striking that, in the United States, one in eleven baby-boomers has joined a demonstration in the past twelve months, but only one in fifteen millennials has done so. In Europe, the picture is a little more mixed: Young respondents are more likely than older ones to have attended protests in the course of the past twelve months, but they do so at lower levels than previous cohorts did at the same age. This decline in political engagement is even more marked for such measures as active membership in new social movements. Participation in humanitarian and human-rights organizations, for example, is about half as high among the young as among older age cohorts. Thus we find that millennials across Western Europe and North America are less engaged than their elders, both in traditional forms of political participation and in oppositional civic activity.

Rising Support for Authoritarian Alternatives

It is clear that citizens today express less of an attachment to liberal democracy, interpret the nature of democracy in a less liberal way, and have less hope of affecting public policy through active participation in the political process than they once did. What is not clear is how serious a warning sign this is for democratic politics and institutions. Dwindling support for, and engagement with, political institutions might simply reflect the fact that liberal democracy no longer faces any serious competition from alternative regime forms. Perhaps the real reason that citizens who came of age after the end of the Cold War do not express the same fervor in supporting liberal democracy is not that they are indifferent toward their system of government, but simply that they have never experienced a real threat to it. Although this optimistic reading may at first seem plausible, it does not square with the fact that explicit support for authoritarian regime forms is also on the rise.

In the past three decades, the share of U.S. citizens who think that it would be a "good" or "very good" thing for the "army to rule"—a patently undemocratic stance—has steadily risen. In 1995, just one in sixteen respondents agreed with that position; today, one in six agree. While those who hold this view remain in the minority, they can no longer be dismissed as a small fringe, especially since there have been similar increases in the number of those who favor a "strong leader who doesn't have to bother with parliament and elections" and those who want experts rather than the government to "take decisions" for the country. Nor is the United States the only country to exhibit this trend. The proportion agreeing that it would be better to have the army rule has risen in most mature democracies, including Germany, Sweden, and the United Kingdom.

Similarly, while 43 percent of older Americans, including those born between the world wars and their baby-boomer children, do not believe that it is legitimate in a democracy for the military to take over when the government is incompetent or failing to do its job, the figure among millennials is much lower at 19 percent.

In Europe, the generation gap is somewhat less stark but equally clear, with 53 percent of older Europeans and only 36 percent of millennials strongly rejecting the notion that a government's incompetence can justify having the army "take over."

Strikingly, such undemocratic sentiments have risen especially quickly among the wealthy. In 1995, the "rich" (defined as deciles 8 to 10 on a ten-point income scale) were the most *opposed* to undemocratic viewpoints, such as the suggestion that their country would be better off if the "army" ruled. Lower-income respondents (defined as deciles 1 to 5) were most in favor of such a proposition. Since then, relative support for undemocratic institutions has reversed. In almost every region, the rich are now more likely than the poor to express approval for "having the army rule." In the United States, for example, only 5 percent of upper-income citizens thought that army rule was a "good" or "very good" idea in the mid-1990s. That figure has since risen to 16 percent. By way of comparison, in Latin America in the mid-1990s, a decade after the return to civilian rule, 21 percent of upper-income respondents still sup- ported military rule. That figure now stands at 33 percent.

The idea that support for military rule has markedly increased among wealthy citizens of long-established liberal democracies is so counterintuitive that it naturally invites skepticism. Yet it is consistent with similar survey items that measure citizens' openness to other authoritarian alternatives. In the United States, among all age cohorts, the share of citizens who believe that it would be better to have a "strong leader" who does not have to "bother with parliament and elections" has also risen over time: In 1995, 24 percent of respondents held this view; by 2011, that figure had increased to 32 percent. Meanwhile, the proportion of citizens who approve of "having experts, not government, make decisions according to what they think is best for the country" has grown from 36 to 49 percent. One reason for these changes is that whereas two decades ago affluent citizens were much more likely than people of lower income groups to defend democratic institutions, the wealthy are now moderately more likely than others to favor a strong leader who can ignore democratic institutions.

Remarkably, the trend toward openness to nondemocratic alternatives is especially strong among citizens who are both young *and* rich. Returning to the question of approval for military rule, in 1995 only 6 percent of rich young Americans (those born since 1970) believed that it would be a "good" thing for the army to take over; today, this view is held by 35 percent of rich young Americans. Nor is the United States an outlier among mature democracies. In Europe in 1995, 6 percent of high-income earners born since 1970 favored the possibility of "army rule"; today, 17 percent of young upper-income Europeans favor it. This is a striking finding: Rising support for illiberal politics is driven not only by the disempowered, middle-aged, and underemployed. Its vocal supporters can also be found among the young, wealthy, and privileged.

While support for military rule among the young and the wealthy may seem like an aberration, their embrace of nondemocratic practices and institutions should not come as a surprise. If we widen the historical lens, we see that, with the exception of a brief period in the late twentieth century, democracy has usually been associated with redistributive demands by the poor and therefore regarded with skepticism by elites. The newfound aversion to democratic institutions among rich citizens in the West may be no more than a return to the historical norm.[6]

Is Democracy Deconsolidating?

One of the key findings of comparative politics is the astonishing stability of wealthy consolidated democracies. In the first years of their existence, both poor and wealthy democracies are vulnerable to regime change. Poor democracies remain in danger even when they have been democratic for a number of years and have successfully changed governments through elections. Democracies that are both wealthy and consolidated, however, appear to be safe: As Adam Przeworski and Fernando Limongi have shown, no consolidated democracy with a GDP per capita of over $6,000 in 1985 international prices has ever collapsed.[7]

This key finding has underwritten an important body of literature on democratization and regime stability, but it has simultaneously occluded an entire area of study. Apparently secure in the knowledge that wealthy consolidated democracies will not experience regime breakdown, political scientists have abstained from pursuing questions that would seem to be among the most fundamental for the discipline: What can empirical indicators tell us about whether rich consolidated democracies are as stable as they were in the past? Do empirical indicators give us reason to believe that seemingly stable democracies may be in trouble? And what might happen if wealthy democracies do eventually start to experience occasional breakdown, as have virtually all other political-regime types in the history of mankind?

In the famous formulation of Juan Linz and Alfred Stepan, democracies are consolidated when they are the "only game in town."[8] This metaphor is as elusive as it is evocative. What does it mean, in concrete terms, for democracy to be the only game in town? In our view, the degree to which a democracy is consolidated depends on three key characteristics: the degree of popular support for democracy as a system of government; the degree to which antisystem parties and movements are weak or nonexistent; and the degree to which the democratic rules are accepted.

This empirical understanding of democratic consolidation opens up conceptual space for the possibility of "democratic deconsolidation." In theory, it is possible that, even in the seemingly consolidated democracies of North America and Western Europe, democracy may one day cease to be the "only game in town": Citizens who once accepted democracy as the only legitimate form of government could become more open to authoritarian alternatives. Stable party systems in which all major forces were once united in support of democracy could enter into phases of extreme instability or witness the meteoric rise of antisystem parties. Finally, rules that were once respected by all important political players could suddenly come under attack by politicians jostling for partisan advantage.

It is at least plausible to think that such a process of democratic deconsolidation may already be underway in a number of established democracies in North America and Western Europe. In the United States, citizens have rapidly lost faith in the political system; in early March 2016, for example, public approval of Congress stood at a mere 13 percent. Wealthy businessman and television personality Donald Trump, having attracted fervent and surprisingly broad support by railing against the political system and promising policies that would openly violate the rights of ethnic and religious minorities, appears to have won the Republican nomination for the presidency of the United States. Meanwhile, even mainstream political actors are increasingly willing to violate the informal rules for the sake of partisan advantage: To name but one example of the resulting gridlock and constitutional dysfunction, the U.S. Senate has refused even to consider President Barack Obama's nominee for a vacant seat on the Supreme Court.

In Europe, too, there have been many signs of democratic deconsolidation in recent years. Approval ratings for the continent's leading politicians stand at record lows, and citizens have grown deeply mistrustful of their political institutions. Far-right populist parties, such as France's National Front or the Sweden Democrats, have risen from obscurity to transform the party system of virtually every Western European country. Meanwhile, parts of Central and Eastern Europe bear witness to the institutional and ideological transformations that might be afoot: In Poland and Hungary, populist strongmen have begun to put pressure on critical media, to violate minority rights, and to undermine key institutions such as independent courts.

To answer the question of whether democracy is deconsolidating in these countries in a rigorous manner would require a research program of considerable breadth that is beyond the scope of a single essay focusing on public-opinion data. But before such a project can get off the ground, an important empirical puzzle needs to be identified and a set of coherent explanatory goals formulated.

If we take the number of people who claim to endorse democracy at face value, no regime type in the history of mankind has held such universal and global appeal as democracy does today. Yet the reality of contemporary democracies looks rather less triumphant than this fact might suggest. Citizens of democracies are less and less content with their institutions; they are more and more willing to jettison institutions and norms that have traditionally been regarded as central components of democracy; and they are increasingly attracted to alternative regime forms.

Far from showing that citizens have merely become more willing to criticize particular governments because their expectations of democracy have grown, this indicates a deep tension at the heart of contemporary politics: Even as democracy has come to be the only form of government widely viewed as legitimate, it has lost the trust of many citizens who no longer believe that democracy can deliver on their most pressing needs and preferences. The optimistic view that this decline in confidence merely represents a temporary downturn is no more than a pleasing assumption, based in part on a reluctance to call into question the vaunted stability of affluent democracies.

Democracies do not die overnight, nor do democracies that have begun to deconsolidate necessarily fail. But we suspect that the degree of democratic consolidation is one of the most important factors in determining the likelihood of democratic breakdown. In a world where most citizens fervently support democracy, where antisystem parties are marginal or nonexistent, and where major political forces respect the rules of the political game, democratic breakdown is extremely unlikely. It is no longer certain, however, that this is the world we live in.

Even if subsequent research should show that democratic deconsolidation really is underway, this would not mean that any particular democracy would soon collapse. Nor is it obvious that the democracy that had deconsolidated the most would be the first to fail. Regime change is always a matter of accident as well as intention, of historical circumstances as well as structural preconditions. But if democratic deconsolidation were proven to be in progress, it would mean that what was once unthinkable should no longer be considered outside the realm of possibility. As democracies deconsolidate, the prospect of democratic breakdown becomes increasingly likely—even in parts of the world that have long been spared such instability. If political scientists are to avoid being blindsided by the demise of established democracies in the coming decades, as they were by the fall of communism a few decades ago, they need to find out whether democratic deconsolidation is happening; to explain the possible causes of this development; to delineate its likely consequences (present and future); and to ponder the potential remedies.

NOTES

1. These gaps remain consistent at other points in the spectrum.
2. Support for radicalism is measured by responses to a left-right political scale, with "1" as radical left and "10" as radical right. In both Europe and North America, self-reported political radicalism is higher among the youngest age cohort (born since 1980) than any previous generation in any previous survey.
3. Andreas Schedler and Rodolfo Sarsfield, "Democrats with Adjectives: Linking Direct and Indirect Measures of Democratic Support," *European Journal of Political Research* 46 (August 2007): 637–59, and Michael Bratton and Robert Mattes, "How People View Democracy: Africans' Surprising Universalism," *Journal of Democracy* (January 2001): 107–21.
4. See Robert A. Dahl, Ian Shapiro, and José Antônio Cheibub, eds., *The Democracy Sourcebook* (Cambridge: MIT Press, 2003); and Alejandro Moreno and Christian Welzel, "Enlightening People: The Spark of Emancipative Values," in Russell J. Dalton and Christian Welzel, eds., *The Civic Culture Transformed: From Allegiant to Assertive Citizens* (New York: Cambridge University Press, 2013).
5. Christian Welzel, *Freedom Rising: Human Empowerment and the Quest for Emancipation* (New York: Cambridge University Press, 2013), Pippa Norris, *Democratic Deficit: Critical Citizens Revisited* (New York: Cambridge University Press, 2011).
6. Two recent contributions to this argument are Carles Boix, *Democracy and Redistribution* (New York: Cambridge University Press, 2003) and Daron Acemoglu and James A. Robinson, *Economic Origins of Dictatorship and Democracy* (New York: Cambridge University Press, 2006).
7. Adam Przeworski et al., *Democracy and Development: Political Institutions and Well-Being in the World, 1950–1990* (New York: Cambridge University Press, 2000).
8. Juan J. Linz and Alfred Stepan, *Problems of Democratic Transition and Consolidation* (Baltimore: Johns Hopkins University Press, 1996).

Periodical and Internet Sources Bibliography

The following articles have been selected to supplement the diverse views presented in this chapter.

Data Team, "Declining Trust in Government Is Denting Democracy," *Economist*, "Daily Chart Blog," January 25, 2017. http://www.economist.com/blogs/graphicdetail/2017/01/daily-chart-20.

Douglas Heaven, "The Uncertain Future of Democracy," BBC.com, March 30, 2017. http://www.bbc.com/future/story/20170330-the-uncertain-future-of-democracy.

Garry Kasparov and Thor Halvorssen, "Why the Rise of Populism Is a Global Catastrophe," *Washington Post,* February 13, 2017.

Chris Lehmann, "Donald Trump and the Long Tradition of American Populism," *Newsweek*, August 22, 2015. http://www.newsweek.com/donald-trump-populism-365052.

Eddie Scarry, "Peggy Noonan: The Democratic Party 'Blowing Itself Up,'" *Washington Examiner*, April 28, 2017. http://www.washingtonexaminer.com/peggy-noonan-democratic-party-blowing-itself-up/article/2621549.

Paul D. Shinkman, "How Vladimir Putin Won the US Election," USNews.com, November 9, 2016. https://www.usnews.com/news/world/articles/2016-11-09/how-vladimir-putin-won-the-us-election.

Benjamin Wallace-Wells, "Trump's Populism Is Not Just a Western Phenomenon," *New Yorker*, November 16, 2016. http://www.newyorker.com/news/benjamin-wallace-wells/trumps-populism-is-not-just-a-western-phenomenon.

Stephen M. Walt, "10 Ways to Tell if Your President Is a Dictator: Just Because the United States Is a Democracy Now, It Doesn't Mean It Will Stay that Way," FP, November 23, 2016. http://foreignpolicy.com/2016/11/23/ten-ways-to-tell-if-your-president-is-a-dictator.

Francis Wilkinson. "Why Donald Trump Really Is a Populist," *Bloomberg View*, February 16, 2017. https://www.bloomberg.com/view/articles/2017-02-16/why-donald-trump-really-is-a-populist.

Chapter 3

Does the US System of Representation Preclude a True Democracy?

Chapter Preface

Much confusion has arisen in recent years when the candidate who won the most votes in the US presidential election did not win the office. The reason this is possible is that the president is not directly elected by the voters but by representatives of the political parties, called "electors," that the voters send to cast ballots on their behalf. Each state is allowed a certain number of electors based on the size of its population. In all but two states, the party that wins the popular vote sends its electors to the meeting of the electoral college. This means that if the loser of the popular vote wins narrowly in states with a large number of electoral votes, he or she can become president, even if the majority of the nation's voters preferred the other candidate.

This system, which seems startlingly anti-democratic today, was designed in part in part to balance the interests of states with large populations and those with small populations, and in part to prevent uninformed voters from electing an unqualified or even nefarious candidate. In the Federalist Paper No. 68, "The Mode of Electing the President," Alexander Hamilton explains that the system is intended to prevent "foreign powers [from gaining] an improper ascendant in our councils" by "raising a creature of their own to the chief magistracy of the Union."

The Electoral College is not the only example of how the US government seems designed to subvert the will of the majority. The allotment of two senators to each state, no matter the population of that state, gives individuals in states with smaller populations a significantly larger say in legislation than citizens in more densely populated states. And, of course monied interests have an outsized influence in many Western Democracies, including the United States.

The viewpoints in this chapter examine the many ways in which the US government is not quite the one-person, one-vote democracy many believe it is—or believe it was designed to be—and how that might be corrected, if indeed it should be corrected.

Viewpoint 1

> *"When the U.S. Constitution was drafted in 1787, the Founding Fathers took pains to ensure the new government would not be a democracy."*

The United States Is Not and Was Never Intended to Be a Democracy

Matt Peppe

In the following viewpoint, Matt Peppe begins by explaining how the United States' image as the exemplar and defender of democracy is used for justification for anything the government chooses to do. He then goes on to discuss what democracy is, how that concept has changed throughout history, and how the United States constitution was specifically designed to not be a democracy. He offers a take on US government in modern times and points to what needs to be done to make the nation a true democracy. Matt Peppe writes about politics and US foreign policy for several Internet sites, including Truthout and CounterPunch.

As you read, consider the following questions:

1. Why, according to Peppe, did the Founding Fathers leave decision-making to a "small, elite group of men"?
2. What in Peppe's view would a true democracy look like?
3. What would have to change for Peppe to believe that the United States is in fact a democracy?

Every one in the world knows that the government of the United States is a democracy, and that the United States stands for promoting democracy around the world. How do we know this is true? Because the government says so, all the time.

"Democracy and respect for human rights have long been central components of U.S. foreign policy," claims the State Department. "Supporting democracy not only promotes such fundamental American values as religious freedom and worker rights, but also helps create a more secure, stable and prosperous global arena in which the United States can advance its national interests."

Idealists would say this is a very benevolent sounding notion. Realists might say it is vacuous and inane. But the media, textbooks, even human rights organizations choose to propagate the idealistic version and claim as an article of faith that the United States does not just practice democracy, but embodies the very idea itself.

Democracy is used as a justification for everything the government does—domestically and abroad. Since the U.S. is the embodiment of democracy and democracy is good, then everything the U.S. does is good, by definition.

But it's not very often that anyone bothers to actually analyze this. Other than being an abstract concept, what actually is democracy and how does the U.S. fit this definition? As most people know, democracy comes from the ancient Greeks. It means power to the people. In Athenian democracy, people participated in governmental decision making by directly participating, with a majority vote used to determine how to act. Even in this system, only free males were granted the right of citizenship and participation in government so it was not a true democracy.

A true democracy would grant voting rights to all citizens —and no one would be denied citizenship because they were considered property. Neither should race, gender, religion, ethnicity or any other factor prevent someone from attaining citizenship and exercising their right to participate in government. In a true democracy, anyone who was subject to the rule of a government —and of adult age—would enjoy the rights of citizenship and democratic participation.

When the U.S. Constitution was drafted in 1787, the Founding Fathers took pains to ensure the new government would not be a democracy. They would create a government that bore some resemblance to democracy, but left the true decision making power in the hands of a small, elite group of men, who were better equipped to rule than the majority of the population.

James Madison, who drafted the document that the final draft of the Constitution was modeled on, made no secret of his disdain for democracy.

"If a faction consists of less than a majority, relief is supplied by the republican principle, which enables the majority to defeat its sinister views by regular vote. It may clog the administration, it may convulse the society; but it will be unable to execute and mask its violence under the forms of the Constitution," Madison wrote in The Federalist No. 10. "When a majority is included in a faction, the form of popular government, on the other hand, enables it to sacrifice to its ruling passion or interest both the public good and the rights of other citizens. To secure the public good and private rights against the danger of such a faction, and at the same time to preserve the spirit and the form of popular government, is then the great object to which our inquiries are directed."

So in other words, the question for the Founding Fathers was how to protect the elites from the tyranny of the majority while maintaining a facade of popular rule? Madison's solution was a "republic, by which I mean a government in which the scheme of representation takes place." A republic, further, would be better at "controlling the effects of faction."

Madison meant that there needed to be a mechanism to control an opinion that was out of the control of elite interest, regardless of whether this opinion belonged to a majority. "By a faction, I understand a number of citizens, whether amounting to a majority or a minority of the whole, who are united and actuated by some common impulse of passion, or of interest, adversed to the rights of other citizens, or to the permanent and aggregate interests of the community."

The Constitution that emerged was able to achieve the delicate balance of some popular representation while keeping the true decision making power within the capable and deserving elite cabal. The House of Representatives would be the minor half of the lawmaking body of Congress. Its members would be elected by popular vote. The Senate would be the truly powerful body, with sole power over foreign policy for example, and that would not be representative. Each state would get 2 Senators, whether that state has 10 residents or 10 million. Further, the Senators would not be elected by the public. They would be chosen by the State Legislatures.

The President, the single most powerful member of the government, would be chosen by the vote of delegations of the State Legislatures. There would be a popular vote, sure, but it is non-binding. So if, for instance, 213 years later a son of a former President lost the popular election he could still become President even though another person had a higher number of votes.

So, fundamentally the U.S. government was designed to *not* be a democracy. It was designed to be a vehicle for white property owners to protect their interests—namely, their property and their right to perpetuate their ownership of it while those with less remained with less.

They would probably be pleased to know that several hundred years later their governmental experiment is fulfilling its purpose to perfection.

In a recent study, researchers at Princeton University and Northwestern University concluded that U.S. policymaking favors the wealthy and special interests groups more than average citizens. In fact, the wishes of average citizens are hardly represented by their elected representatives, if at all.

"Not only do ordinary citizens not have *uniquely* substantial power over policy decisions; they have little or no independent influence on policy at all," write Martin Gilens and Benjamin Page.

"We believe that if policymaking is dominated by powerful business organizations and a small number of affluent Americans, then America's claims to being a democratic society are seriously threatened," they conclude.

Of course, a look at the historical record showed this was actual the intent of the Founding Fathers all along.

Maybe because of the transparent lack of actual democratic mechanisms and institutions, the United States eventually began to narrow the definition of democracy essentially to one thing: the right to vote.

William Blum writes that this sense of the word was developed as propaganda to criticize Communist governments who considered things such as food, health care and education fundamental human rights. But they didn't have regular elections. So our system, with its glorious box checking, became "democracy" while theirs was "totalitarianism," Blum explains.

"Thus, a nation with hordes of hungry, homeless, untended sick, barely literate, unemployed, and/or tortured people, whose loved ones are being disappeared and/or murdered with state connivance, can be said to be living in a 'democracy' … provided that every two years or four years they have the right to go to a designated place and put an X next to the name of one or another individual who promises to relieve their miserable condition, but who will, typically, do virtually nothing of the kind."

It has taken an Orwellian perversion of the English language to claim that countries like Venezuela and Cuba, who practice versions of grassroots, direct democratic groups like people's councils and trade unions, are not part of democracy if they don't have multi-party elections.

As this is really the sole basis of U.S. claims to democracy you would think it would be a valid claim. But you would be wrong. The truth is that in the history of the nation, there has not been even *one single day* where all voting-age United States citizens were allowed to vote in federal elections!

At the time of the Constitution, only land-owning white males were allowed to vote. This obviously left out landless whites, all women, and all African Americans. This was true until the Civil War.

"In 1860, just five states limited suffrage to taxpayers and only two still imposed property qualifications," writes Steven Mintz.

So at this point, no African Americans or women had the right to vote. Shortly after, with the ratification of the Fifteenth Amendment, African Americans were granted the nominal right to vote. However, poll taxes, literacy tests and other obstacles were used especially in the South to ensure that freed slaves were not able to exercise that right—at least in more than small numbers. It was not until the Civil Rights Act in 1964 that this type of disenfranchisement was federally prohibited.

Meanwhile, between the passage of the 15th amendment in 1870 and the passage of the 19th amendment in 1920, no women were allowed to vote.

But even still, there was another group of citizens that could not—and still cannot—vote. U.S. nationals of foreign colonies acquired in 1898 were never granted the right to vote in federal elections. The largest group of these colonial subjects, Puerto Ricans, were even granted citizenship in 1917 with the passage of the Jones Act. Woodrow Wilson was kind enough to sign the law that would grant Puerto Ricans the privilege of citizenship. They would then be allowed to be drafted into military service, so they could die for the United States in World War I.

So even after women attained suffrage in 1920, no U.S. citizens of Puerto Rico or nationals of other colonies have ever been able to vote. All the other current colonies—Guam, U.S. Virgin Islands, American Samoa and the Northern Mariana Islands—later did receive citizenship. Together with the 3.6 million residents of Puerto Rico, they number nearly 4 million U.S. citizens who were not able to cast a vote for or against Barack Obama but have to call him their President.

They are not able to vote on adopting a universal health care system, paid parental leave, or paid vacation for all U.S. citizens —or any other policy in line with the rest of the developed world. They are not able to have a vote on free trade treaties, funding to Israel, or anything else that is decided on the federal level by the rest of the United States citizens.

Even within the States themselves, millions of citizens who have been convicted of felonies are denied the right to vote for the rest of their lives. Michelle Alexander points out the similarities to the discriminatory system that reigned in the South until the Civil Rights Act in her book "The New Jim Crow: Mass Incarceration in the Age of Colorblindness".

Most often, the people receiving felony convictions are poor black and Latinos who have committed non-violent drug offenses disproportionately enforced on those communities. Even in the case of violent offenders, the question begs itself whether the commission of a crime, which is paid for by the perpetrator in the form of imprisonment, merits a lifetime ban from voting. Is it fair to enforce discriminatory policies and then cut the victims of these policies off from the only avenue they have to change them?

Maybe someday Americans will decide that to meet even the minimal qualifications of democracy that exist in the U.S., all citizens must have the right to vote.

> *"A* real *democracy, however, is a direct and participatory democracy, in which all citizens have the possibility and the right to participate in the decisions that affect our lives and our communities."*

Real Democracy Takes Active Participation on the Part of Citizens

Camilla Hansen

In the following viewpoint, author Camilla Hansen agrees that the United States' system of government is not really a democracy—nor are most Western democracies. She argues that the perpetual cycling of parties and politicians will not fix the problems with modern republics. What is needed, she says, is a change of governments—to true democracies. This would require far more than citizens who vote periodically, however, and she paints a picture of what a true participatory democracy would look like. Hansen is a democracy activist who lives in Oslo, Norway.

"What Would Real Democracy Look Like?" by Camilla Hansen, New Compass, July 29, 2013. Reprinted by permission.

As you read, consider the following questions:

1. What, according to this author, are the problems with current republics?
2. How does a true democracy differ from a democratic republic, and why does Hansen think that difference is important?
3. Hansen's proposals are complex and would be time-consuming for citizens. Why does she say they are worth the difficulties involved?

Today, democracy is equated with representative government based on free elections of political elites that rule on the citizens' behalf. This system, referred to as "representative democracy," has been the dominant one in the West for the last two hundred years and is now being exported across the world and promoted as the only possible alternative to outright dictatorship.

But this system is now in a deep crisis. In established representative democracies, the trust in political elites and conventional institutions is crumbling. Participation in elections is shrinking, and political parties are loosing their members. In the old "well-developed democracies" of Europe, the streets are boiling as millions protest against unpopular and brutal austerity policies imposed on them from above. More and more people are now realizing that their elected representatives do not represent them. Rather, governments of both left and right bow to the dictates of the big banks, the financial institutions and the multinational corporations and their powerful lobbies. In this situation, the ballot has little meaning because we have no real choice. We can only change political elites that rule us, but we do not have the right to decide upon the development of the society in which we live.

A *real* democracy, however, is a direct and participatory democracy, in which all citizens have the possibility and the right to participate in the decisions that affect our lives and our communities. While the powers that be and mainstream media and pundits argue that such a citizen-based democracy is not possible or even desirable, there exist in fact a range of new institutions and experiments—as well as some old ones - that show that a direct and participatory democracy is both possible and feasible today. These democratic innovations, however scattered and limited, could, if improved, strengthened and spread, be tools for a radical democratisation of society. In this article I will take a look at some of these democratic institutions and mechanisms, discuss their strengths and weaknesses, and explore their potentials.

Participatory Budgeting

The popular assembly where citizens meet face to face to discuss, vote and make collective decisions is the original form of democracy. Historically different kinds of popular assemblies have existed in many communities across the world, from village assemblies in North Africa to the Assembly of ancient Athens, the Landsgemeinde of the medieval Swiss cantons, and the town meetings of 17th century New England.[1] The recent decades a myriad of new democratic institutions have been created across the world, in which popular assemblies form an essential part of the institutional structure. The most famous of these is participatory budgeting.

Participatory budgeting lets residents decide how to spend their city's or municipality's public budget through a process of popular assemblies in the neighbourhoods and the districts. It was first developed in the city of Porto Alegre in Southern Brazil in the late 1980s when the Brazilian Labour Party, PT, won the municipal elections after the end of the military dictatorship. Since then, it has spread to hundreds of cities and municipalities in Latin America, Europe and the United States.

In the neighbourhood assemblies all residents have the right to participate and to vote on the budget priorities of their neighbourhood. These assemblies then elect delegates to regional assemblies and to a budget council, which puts together a budget for the whole city, based on the priorities made in the neighbourhood assemblies. Large numbers participate in the process; in some places over 100,000 participate each year. Usually the majority of the participants are women, poor and other sections of the population that are marginalized in conventional political institutions. Participatory budgeting has lead to many positive results, including poverty reduction and redistribution of budget resources to the poorest neighbourhoods, a large reduction in corruption, and to more transparency as well as a more vibrant civil society.

However, there are large variations in the institutional design of the different models of participatory budgeting that have spread across the world. The strong models give the residents decision-making power over the entire or large parts of the municipal budget and are based on neighbour assemblies where all residents can participate and vote on priorities. It is these strong models that have produced the best results in the form of poverty reduction, decline in corruption and large participation from the residents.[2]

In the original model of participatory budgeting that was created in Porto Alegre, several rules were built into the process that encouraged participation and ensured transparency and accountability. The more residents that participated in a certain neighbourhood assembly, the more delegates that neighbourhood got in the regional forums that could argue for their neighbourhood's priorities. This mechanism mobilized many, especially from the poor and marginalized neighbourhoods to participate.[3] Additionally, the municipal administration hired community organizers that informed the residents about the process and encouraged people to participate. To prevent the establishment of a professionalized political class, all delegates were recallable and their terms were limited and short (1–2 years). The mayor and the municipal administration participated in the meetings, so that the residents could hold them to account. And to ensure transparency, all meetings were open to the public and all information was made accessible.

A major dilemma of participatory budgeting is the question of legislative power. In Venezuela[4] and Peru[5] participatory budgeting is mandatory for all the countries' municipalities by national law. Most cases of participatory budgeting around the world though, have no direct legislative power. In Porto Alegre, participatory budgeting was not codified into the municipal law. The reason for this was to keep it flexible and this made it possible to gradually expand the process to give citizen power over larger parts of the budget. On the other hand, when participatory budgeting is not codified into law, the municipal administration can abolish or restructure the process at any time.[6] Thus, the process gets vulnerable to governments and politicians wanting to undermine it by reducing citizens' decision-making power and participation.

Participatory budgeting, as it was first conceived of in Porto Alegre, is also facing other challenges. As Carole Pateman documents in her essay "Participatory Democracy Revisited", many of the institutional models that are being promoted as participatory budgeting bear very little resemblance to the original Porto Alegre model.[7] These are models where citizens either have decision-making power over only a tiny fraction of the budget or some small additional funds, or where citizens only have an advisory role and no decision-making power. As weak models have been promoted by international agencies like the World Bank, the term participatory budgeting has been emptied of content. It is now being used to cover any kind of participation, including consultation, information sharing or giving feedback to government. Also in Porto Alegre itself, the process has become diluted the last decade.

If participatory budgeting is to be a tool for genuine democratisation of society, the citizens must be given decision-making power over the entire or at least a large part of the municipal budget, and the process must be a bottom-up process where the sovereign power lies with the citizens in the assemblies. Local authorities must be willing to give away power to the residents in the assemblies, and there is a need for decentralization of power from national and international levels to the municipal and local levels. This latter happened in Brazil, as the country's constitution of 1988 moved considerable power to the municipalities, including economic power.[8]

Communal Councils

Another participatory institution based on popular assemblies is the "consejos comunales", the communal councils in Venezuela. Communal councils are small local participatory institutions, composed of approximately 200-400 families in urban areas and 20-50 families in rural areas, which make decisions about initiation and implementation of local projects. Projects include basic services like water and sewage systems, electricity, medical centres, housing and road building, as well as cultural activities. All decisions are made through popular assemblies composed of at least 10 percent of residents over 15 years. The assemblies also elect committees tasked with financial management, monitoring of government, and local priorities like health, education and land management.[9]

In a few years, the communal councils have become very popular, and there are now over 30,000 of them across Venezuela. The government has transferred billions of dollars to the councils, and thousands of projects have been implemented. Also, larger 'communes' have been created, consisting of many communal councils.

As with participatory budgeting in Brazil, decentralization was a crucial step in moving power downwards to ordinary citizens at the grassroots level. Although The Communal Councils Law was passed in 2006, a decentralization process started already in the 1980s, paved the way. Through this process, considerable power was moved from national and regional levels to municipal governments. In 2006, the decentralization was continued and deepened by the Chavez government, by moving power further down, from local governments to the citizens in the neighbourhoods.[10]

However, the communal councils still have to apply to the Presidential Commission of Popular Power for funding. This gives the central government in Caracas the final power to decide which projects will be funded. National agencies also determine the rules which guide the communal councils and these rules limit the power of the councils. The communal councils have met opposition both from local and national bureaucracy, and the national government has been criticized for trying to centralize and dominate the process.

None of these weaknesses are unfixable; the communal councils have potential to be strengthened and further democratised. Council participants and social movements are actively struggling to take power back from the central government to the communities and are demanding more power over funding, rules and other parts of the process. Innovative proposals to decentralize and radicalise the communal council system have also appeared, including a proposal to integrate different levels of government through "popular federalism"; "a state where regional autonomy is strong and the central state weak, but coordinating." This proposal is a model of participatory democracy that would compose a multi-level system of participation.

Participatory budgeting and communal councils are two of the most well known cases of participatory institutions in which popular assemblies play a key role. There exists, however, a large number of other institutions, ranging from the Zapatistas' Councils of Good Government and the Kurdish general assemblies and councils, to the neighbourhood assemblies and committees making decisions on cultural policies and urban planning in Grottamare, Italy; participatory municipal administration in Camaragibe, Brazil; and worker-owned cooperatives in Argentina and elsewhere. By studying these institutions, we can identify their strengths and limitations; how they can be improved and spread; and in which ways they can contribute to a radical democratisation of society.

Sortition and Mini-publics

Certain democratic mechanisms are essential to participatory institutions, as they prevent the establishment of a cemented and professionalized political class insulated from ordinary citizens and local communities. Such mechanisms include short and limited terms for elected delegates, and delegates being recallable at any time. Rotation of delegates is another way to prevent creation of elites and to ensure diversity and mass participation. In the Zapatistas' Councils of Good Government, for example, each citizen serves on the Council for only two weeks, before they go back to their communities.

Another mechanism that effectively prevents establishment of elites and ensures the participation of ordinary citizens in decision-making and as holders of political offices, is sortition, or selection by lot. The use of lot played an important role in the democracy of ancient Athens, where most positions of political authority were selected this way. For Aristotle, selection by lot was central to democracy, while elections were the mark of oligarchy. In the Athenian democracy, lot ensured that citizens could "rule and be ruled in turn", and together with rotation of office, it functioned as a defence against oligarchy. In modern representative systems, however, selection by lot is absent. "Democracy" is now exclusively equated with competitive elections for positions of political authority.[11]

However, the last decades there has been a range of experiments with sortition in deliberative institutions like citizens' assemblies, citizen juries, consensus conferences, planning cells and deliberative polls, often referred to as mini-publics. Sortition was also recently used in the first part of the process to write a new constitution in Iceland.

In mini-publics, deliberation is usually guided by independent facilitators; the participants hold hearings in which they hear evidence from and question expert witnesses; and deliberations usually take place both in plenary and in small groups. Participants are selected for mini-publics through the use of statistical sampling to ensure that citizens from all social groups are represented. Sortition differs from popular assemblies in that equal *opportunity* to participate is replaced by equal *probability* to being selected to participate. This way, no citizens or social groups are systemically excluded from participation.[12]

With a few exceptions, like the British Columbia Citizens Assembly, most mini-publics are only advisory. The participating citizens are consulted, but they don't have any decision making power. Another weakness of most mini-publics is the role of organizers (usually governments), who set the agenda and choose experts and thus are able to influence the outcome of the deliberations. In this way mini-publics can be manipulated by existing political institutions and elites to legitimise decisions made elsewhere. And, as Pateman points out, most mini-publics are only temporary and are usually advocated as a mere supplement to the existing electoral system.[13]

Experiments with mini-publics and recent use of sortition, however, have given us rich proofs that ordinary citizens are able discuss and solve complex problems when given the possibility to do so and that they are able to take important decisions in the public interest. Several democratic theorists have recently made proposals for different kinds of political bodies, including legislative bodies, based on sortition that would not just be complements to the existing electoral institutions, but constitute alternatives.

Citizens Initiatives

Citizen initiatives are democratic mechanisms that let citizens propose and vote on laws and policies. By gathering a certain amount of signatures, citizens can demand a binding vote on a proposed policy or legislation. Citizen initiatives differ from referendums in which citizens only can accept or reject a law or policy proposed by parliament. Switzerland was the first country to introduce citizen initiatives as well as referendums, and several countries, especially in Europe and Latin America have since introduced them at national, state or local levels.

The promise of citizen initiatives is the way in which they can give citizens power to initiate and to directly decide upon large-scale issues. But like the other democratic institutions and mechanisms discussed above, citizen initiatives also have their limitations. A common problem is that the large numbers of signatures required and the short time frame ensure that only those who can afford to use expensive professional signature-gathering firms can submit an initiative.

Another problem is that citizen initiatives are often subverted by the manipulations of wealthy and powerful interests and political elites. Big business frequently pours huge sums of money into misleading campaigns to influence the outcome of the vote (a recent example of this is the proposition 37 to label food containing GMOs in California that was defeated by agribusiness which spent 45 million dollars on misleading ad campaigns). It is also common that corporations and corporate lobbies launch counter-initiatives to defeat initiatives on social or environmental issues that they don't like.

This does not mean that citizen initiatives cannot be valuable democratic tools, but there is a need for careful consideration of how these are designed, to prevent their subversion by the wealthy and the powerful. Improvements could include lower number of signatures required and longer timelines, and eliminating campaign contributions. Also it is important to ensure that citizens get sufficient information about the issues to be voted upon and to ensure a broad and inclusive public deliberation.

Citizen initiatives are effective instruments for decision, but not for deliberation. While direct democracy also should include other tools and arenas for decision making than popular assemblies, a system based mainly on voting would be atomistic and insufficient. In face-to-face assemblies and other forms of collective decision-making, citizens are exposed to and required to recognize and take into consideration the views of other citizens with different perspectives and backgrounds and are thus better able to make considered judgements.[14] But in spite of their limitations, citizen initiatives can constitute an important element in a broader framework of diverse direct democratic and participatory institutions.

A Grassroots Network for Participatory Democracy

A radical direct and participatory democracy will not be handed down to us by the elites, but has to be struggled for by ordinary citizens and social movements. As Occupy Oakland activists Gabriel Hetland and Abigail N. Martin emphasize, institutional reforms must be accompanied by popular struggle and direct action. This is exactly what happened in the municipality of Torres in Venezuela, where hundreds of citizens occupied City Hall to demand implementation of participatory budgeting. The result of this popular struggle was one of the world's best participatory budgets, in which residents have control over 100 percent of the municipal investment budget.

For a radical democratic change to happen, there must be large popular movements demanding and struggling for this change. But unless ideas of direct and participatory democracy are known and familiar to most people, such movements will not emerge. So a first step then, is to spread these ideas and make a strong argument for how direct and participatory democracy can be feasible today. As Kristinn Már Ársælsson from the democratic association ALDA in Iceland points out, people will not call for what they don't know.

Perhaps the time has come to create an international network from the bottom-up of social movements and activists campaigning for and struggling for direct and participatory democracy. While there already exist some networks and initiatives, most of these are sponsored by or supported by agencies like the World Bank and by governments and other elite institutions. Few of these aim for participatory institutions as tools for radical democratisation, but see these as mere additions to the existing political system. What is lacking is a more radical agenda, an international grassroots-based network promoting and struggling for participatory democracy as an alternative and ultimately a replacement to the existing system. Through such a network, social movements, activists and ordinary citizens across the world could exchange ideas and experiences, learn from each other, and develop common campaigns and struggles.

The huge task of reinventing and struggling for direct and participatory democracy in the age of austerity, centralized corporate power and technocratic rule will not be easy. But in the face of increasing ecological, social, political and economic crises, creating *real* democracy could be our only hope.

Notes

1. Some of these assemblies and town meetings still exist today, but their power has been dramatically reduced as most decision making power has been moved away from local and municipal levels to national and international levels.
2. Pateman, Carole. (2012), "Participatory Democracy Revisited", *Perspectives on Politics* 10, p. 12.
3. Smith, Graham. (2009) *Democratic Innovations: Designing Institutions for Citizen Participation*, New York: Cambridge University Press, p. 43.
4. Hetland, Gabriel. (2012) "Grassroots Democracy in Venezuela", http://www.geo.coop/node/782.
5. UN-HABITAT (2004), *72 Frequently Asked Question about Participatory Budgeting*, Quite: AH Editorial. Can be downloaded from: http://www.unhabitat.org/documents/faqqPP.pdf.
6. Smith, op. cit., p. 49.
7. Pateman, op. cit., p. 14.
8. Smith, op. cit., p. 65.
9. Lerner, Josh. (2007), "Communal Councils in Venezuela: Can 200 Families Revolutionize Democracy?", http://venezuelanalysis.com/analysis/2257.
10. *Ibid.*
11. Manin, Bernard. (1997), *The Principles of Representative Government*, New York: Cambridge University Press, p. 3.
12. Smith, op. cit., p. 79.
13. Pateman, op. cit., p. 9.
14. Smith, op.cit., 24.

Viewpoint 3

> *"The time has come to stand up to our fathers."*

We Need to Return the Power of Government to the People

Jeffrey Fuller

In the following viewpoint, Jeffrey Fuller begins by pointing out that the Founding Fathers did not intend for everyone to take part in the US democracy. In order to make sure that everyone has a voice in government, he argues that we need to overturn Citizens United, *taking away the right of corporations to be treated as individuals when it comes to political activity. We must also change the way representation is allotted in Congress, and loosen the hold of the two-party system on American politics. Fuller is a teacher and lives in Portland, Oregon.*

As you read, consider the following questions:

1. Would Fuller agree with the previous viewpoints that the US government was not designed to be a democracy?
2. How, according to Fuller, do legal decisions regarding corporate personhood weaken democracy?
3. How does Fuller think that changing the method of Congressional representation would help restore democracy in the United States?

Along with much of the country, I have followed the growing Occupy Wall St. protests this past month. As a supporter of their cause to end corporate greed and level the economic playing field, I have also read closely the criticisms of the movement. Some of those appear little more than the scared exclamations recently outlined in Paul Krugman's *New York Times* editorial, "Panic of the Plutocracy."

But the protests go well beyond the "rigged" economic system Krugman discusses and from which the movement has seemingly developed. What it demands, at its very core, is a change in our government's structure to adequately represent the people of United States.

It is true that many of our Founding Fathers feared real democracy for all the people. The poor, the uneducated, and the landless classes, not to mention women and minorities, were not to be trusted with the power of voting, and in many cases, were excluded from juries or testifying in court. One aspect of the Electoral College was to remove from the people the ability to elect the President directly. That power, instead, was given to the individual states, forming our federal republic.

The time has come to stand up to our fathers, both Founding and those that came in subsequent generations. We must tell them that while their grand test in democracy was a truly defining time in human history, while many of their ideals still hold as true today as they did over 200 years ago, others have failed us, have been manipulated and become diseased. It is time we step beyond those principles that have proven incapable of protecting our inalienable rights and evolve into a truer democracy that caters to our whole populace.

One of the first steps in re-democratizing the United States is to rewrite the laws regarding corporate personhood as defined by the U.S. Supreme Court in 1886 and extended by future courts, including the current Roberts court in the Citizen's United decision. While corporations clearly need rights regarding contracts, they neither deserve nor need further rights giving them virtually every power extended to human citizens beyond the literal ballot box.

Within this, corporations and their lobbying organizations should be eliminated, or at the very least significantly limited, from the halls of congress. Corporate money in elections does nothing for our democracy or the good of the people but to expand the already bulging pockets of their CEOs and major stockholders. The individual votes of their employees and stockholders, should they chose to cast them, give individual corporations plenty of power at the ballot box as is. The additional financial flooding of elections is both unnecessary and dangerous to our democracy.

A second necessity comes in reforming how we the people are represented within our government. The Reappointment Act of 1929 fixed the number of House of Representative members at 435. Till then, the number of House reps grew along with the census, allowing voters easier access to their representative and allowing for a more representative congress. Today, each HoR member averages over 700,000 constituents, a number far too large (and growing) for anyone to believe honestly in their ability to find even a modicum of consensus from their constituencies.

Furthermore, the number of congressional members plays a direct role in the number of Electoral College votes allotted each state. As a federal republic of states in which the states themselves are given the power to elect the president and thereby separating the populace from the office directly, the number of House reps plays a vital part in allowing the people's voice to be heard in presidential elections.

In order to more adequately ensure the people's wants are acknowledged properly, we must eliminate from the individual states the power to draw their U.S. House of Representative congressional districts without federal oversight. Party politics at the state level currently control these redistricting efforts, all but eliminating any sense of equal voter distribution within districts. What we are given then is not a fair and balanced division of the people, but gerrymandered districts, which minimize the electability of opponents of the party in power and maximize that of their own.

Rather, when time comes for the federal districts to be redrawn and/or the number of districts is to be expanded or reduced according to population changes, federal law should dictate that non-partisan groups should be given the responsibility of evenly and fairly dividing up the electorate.

There is still, however, a yet untouched problem that has stifled our democracy for well over a century: we must destroy the stranglehold of the two-party system. Everyone knows the well-worn Max Lerner quote, "When you choose between the lesser of two evils, always remember that it is still evil." Yet how many of us continually feel disgust when we vote for our congressional leaders and president that we are left with just that choice?

There is one tested way in which it is easy to usher in new parties and give them the opportunity to run and grow within the political system without being forced to play the role of spoiler. Instant Runoff Voting gives voters the opportunity to rank the candidates according to their preference. If a voter's number one choice finishes last, their second (if listed) most preferred candidate then receives their vote until one candidate stands with at least 50 percent of the vote. The candidates that best represent the people and their interests are therefore elected to hold our most powerful offices.

While these changes are just a beginning in how we must reshape our democracy, while they only touch at the base levels of the changes we must demand, and while this discussion merely lists them and does not detail their implementation, they are a starting point to democratic reform that need be fulfilled.

We must return to the people the power to govern. Corporations, special interests, and the currently unbreakable strength of the two-party system have led us into an oligarchical system in which the people are struggling to maintain even a sliver of a voice at the ballot box. This is unacceptable and outdated. It is time to evolve, to become the great democracy we claim to be.

> "The Senate is
> already undemocratic."

The US Senate Gives Citizens in States with Small Populations an Unfair Advantage

Corey Robin

In the following viewpoint, Corey Robin explains the history behind the peculiar way US Senate representation works. According to Robin, the United States senate is one of the least democratic aspects of the US government. Through his admiration of previous writings, the author asserts that Senate representation has subverted democracy from the beginning, when it was one of the most powerful protections of slavery and Jim Crow. Robin is professor of political science at Brooklyn College and the CUNY Graduate Center, and author of several scholarly books on political science and history.

As you read, consider the following questions:

1. How did the particular arrangements made by the US Constitution enable slavery and racism, according to Robin?
2. Why might the framers of the Constitution been concerned to protect the voices of slave-holding states?
3. How, according to this viewpoint, have the demographics of small and large states shifted in modern times?

"The US Senate: Where Democracy Goes to Die," by Corey Robin, crookedtimber.org, March 12, 2013. Reprinted by permission.

Every once in a while I teach constitutional law, and when I do, I pose to my students the following question: What if the Senate apportioned votes not on the basis of states but on the basis of race? That is, rather than each state getting two votes in the Senate, what if each racial or ethnic group listed in the US Census got two votes instead?

Regardless of race, almost all of the students freak out at the suggestion. It's undemocratic, they cry! When I point out that the Senate is already undemocratic—the vote of any Wyomian is worth vastly more than the vote of each New Yorker—they say, yeah, but that's different: small states need protection from large states. And what about historically subjugated or oppressed minorities, I ask? Or what about the fact that one of the major intellectual moves, if not completely successful coups, of Madison and some of the Framers was to disaggregate or disassemble the interests of a state into the interests of its individual citizens. As Ben Franklin said at the Constitutional Convention, "The Interest of a State is made up of the interests of its individual members. If they are not injured, the State is not injured." The students are seldom moved.

Then I point out that the very opposition they're drawing—between representation on the basis of race versus representation on the basis of states—is itself confounded by the history of the ratification debate over the Constitution and the development of slavery and white supremacy in this country.

As Jack Rakove argued in *Original Meanings*, one of the reasons some delegates from large states ultimately came around to the idea of protecting the interests of small states was that they realized that an equal, if not more powerful, interest than mere population size bound delegate to delegate, state to state: slavery. Virginia had far more in common with South Carolina than it did with Massachussets, a fact that later events would go onto confirm. In Rakove's words:

> The more the delegates examined the apportionment of the lower house [which resulted in the infamous 3/5 clause], the more weight they gave to considerations of regional security.

> Rather than treat sectional differences as an alternative and superior description of the real interests at play in American politics, the delegates saw them instead as an additional conflict that had to be accommodated in order for the Union to endure. The apportionment issue confirmed the claims that the small states had made all along. It called attention not to the way in which an extended republic could protect all interests but to the need to safeguard the conspicuous interest of North and South. This defensive orientation in turn enabled even some large-state delegates to find merit in an equal-state vote.

As Madison, a firm opponent of representation by states, would argue at the Convention:

> It seemed now to be pretty well understood that the real difference of interests lay, not between large and small but between the Northern and Southern States. The institution of slavery and its consequences formed the line of discrimination.

True, Madison made this claim in the service of his argument against representation by states, but for others, his claim pushed in the opposite direction: a pluralism of interests in an extensive republic was not, as Madison claimed in *Federalist* 10, enough to protect the interests of a wealthy propertied minority. Something more—the protection of group interests in the Senate—was required. (Which is why, incidentally, I'm always amused by conservatives' horror at the notion of group rights: what do they think the Senate is all about if not the protection of group rights? This is not to say that there aren't principled reasons to oppose group rights; I'm commenting merely on the scandalized tone of the opposition.)

And when one considers how critical the Senate has been to the protection of both slavery and Jim Crow—measures against both institutions repeatedly passed the House, only to be stymied in the Senate, where the interests of certain types of minorities are more protected than others—the distinction between race and state size becomes even harder to sustain. Though the Senate often gets held up as *the* institution for the protection of minority rights

The End of Democracy

The predators in Washington are only this far from monopoly control of our government. They have bought the political system, lock, stock and pork barrel, making change from within impossible. To them belong the spoils of a looted city. They get the tax breaks, the loopholes, the contracts, the payoffs.

They fix the system so multimillionaire hedge fund managers and private equity tycoons pay less of a tax rate on their income than school teachers, police and fire fighters, secretaries and janitors. They give subsidies to rich corporate farms and cut food stamps for working people facing hunger. They remove oversight of the wall street casinos, bail out the bankers who torpedo the economy, fight the modest reforms of Dodd-Frank, prolong tax havens for multinationals, and stick it to consumers while rewarding corporations.

We pay. We pay at the grocery store. We pay at the gas pump. We pay the taxes they write off. Our low-wage workers pay with sweat and deprivation because this town – aloof, self-obsessed, bought off and doing very well, thank you – feels no pain.

The journalists who could tell us these things rarely do – and some, never. They aren't blind, simply bedazzled. Watch the evening news – any evening news – or the Sunday talk shows. Listen to the chit-chat of the early risers on morning TV — and ask yourself if you are learning anything about how this town actually works.

Perhaps they don't ask these questions because they fear banishment from the parties and perks, from the access that passes as seduction in this town.

Or perhaps they do not tell us these things because they fear that if the system were exposed for what it is, outraged citizens would descend on this town, and tear it apart with their bare hands.

"The End Game for Democracy," by Bill Moyers, Paideia LLC, August 23, 2013.

against majoritarian tyranny, the minorities it protects are often not the powerless or the dissenters of yore and lore.

Indeed, for all the justified disgust with Emory University President James Wagner's recent celebration of the 3/5 Clause, virtually no one ever criticizes the Senate, even though its contribution to the maintenance of white supremacy, over the long course of American history, has been far greater than the 3/5 Clause, which was nullified by the 14th Amendment.

This is all by way of a long introduction to a terrific article in the *New York Times* by Adam Liptak on just this issue of the undemocratic nature of the Senate, and some of the racial dimensions of that un-democracy. Just a few excerpts:

> Vermont's 625,000 residents have two United States senators, and so do New York's 19 million. That means that a Vermonter has 30 times the voting power in the Senate of a New Yorker just over the state line — the biggest inequality between two adjacent states. The nation's largest gap, between Wyoming and California, is more than double that.
>
> The difference in the fortunes of Rutland and Washington Counties reflects the growing disparity in their citizens' voting power, and it is not an anomaly. The Constitution has always given residents of states with small populations a lift, but the size and importance of the gap has grown markedly in recent decades, in ways the framers probably never anticipated. It affects the political dynamic of issues as varied as gun control, immigration and campaign finance.
>
> In response, lawmakers, lawyers and watchdog groups have begun pushing for change. A lawsuit to curb the small-state advantage in the Senate's rules is moving through the courts. The Senate has already made modest changes to rules concerning the filibuster, which has particularly benefited senators from small states. And eight states and the District of Columbia have endorsed a proposal to reduce the chances that the small-state advantage in the Electoral College will allow a loser of the popular vote to win the presidency.
>
> …

> What is certain is that the power of the smaller states is large and growing. Political scientists call it a striking exception to the democratic principle of "one person, one vote." Indeed, they say, the Senate may be the least democratic legislative chamber in any developed nation.
>
> . . .
>
> Behind the growth of the advantage is an increase in population gap between large and small states, with large states adding many more people than small ones in the last half-century. There is a widening demographic split, too, with the larger states becoming more urban and liberal, and the smaller ones remaining rural and conservative, which lends a new significance to the disparity in their political power.
>
> The threat of the filibuster in the Senate, which has become far more common than in past decades, plays a role, too. Research by two political scientists, Lauren C. Bell and L. Marvin Overby, has found that small-state senators, often in leadership positions, have amplified their power by using the filibuster more often than their large-state counterparts.
>
> Beyond influencing government spending, these shifts generally benefit conservative causes and hurt liberal ones. When small states block or shape legislation backed by senators representing a majority of Americans, most of the senators on the winning side tend to be Republicans, because Republicans disproportionately live in small states and Democrats, especially African-Americans and Latinos, are more likely to live in large states like California, New York, Florida and Illinois. Among the nation's five smallest states, only Vermont tilts liberal, while Alaska, Wyoming and the Dakotas have each voted Republican in every presidential election since 1968.

The article is long, but it's worth the entire read. A model of how good journalism can incorporate the insights of historical and institutionalist political science (and not just the number-crunching kind).

VIEWPOINT 5

> *"It's tough to argue with a straight face that this bizarre system is inherently better than just a simple vote."*

We're Stuck with a Lousy System

Andrew Prokop

In the following viewpoint, Andrew Prokop explains what the US Electoral College is, how it works, and why he believes it is a singularly poor idea. If few people are aware of just how undemocratic the US Senate is, far more people feel that way about the Electoral College—and those who weren't already aware, learned quickly after Donald Trump's stunning upset presidential win in 2016. The author argues that the popular vote would be much more democratic, since under the Electoral College system the winner is chosen by residents of just a few states. Prokop covers politics for Vox media.

As you read, consider the following questions:

1. Why, according to Prokop, do defenders of the Electoral College say it works just fine?
2. How, in the electoral college system, does winning New York differ from winning Florida?
3. What are the arguments for the Electoral College system and how does Prokop counter these?

"Why the Electoral College is the absolute worst, explained," by Andrew Prokop, Vox Media, December 19, 2016. http://www.vox.com/policy-and-politics/2016/11/7/12315574/electoral-college-explained-presidential-elections-2016. Reprinted by permission.

Hillary Clinton won more votes than Donald Trump in last month's presidential election. But due to the magic of the Electoral College, Donald Trump will be the next president of the United States.

Yes, the November 8 "presidential election" was in actuality the venerable ritual in which the residents of Florida, Ohio, Pennsylvania, and a few other states got the privilege of choosing the president of the United States of America.

Or, to be more precise, it was the venerable ritual in which all the states chose their representatives in the *Electoral College*. It's those people who are going to technically pick the president this Monday.

It's a patchwork Frankenstein's monster of a system, which in the best of times merely ensures millions of Americans' votes are irrelevant to the outcome because they don't live in competitive states, and in the worst of times could be vulnerable to a major crisis.

Amazingly enough, though, nothing in the Constitution gives American voters the right to choose their president. That power is reserved for those 538 *actual people* who will meet in their respective states this Monday—the electors. It's up to the states to decide how to appoint them.

Despite the oddness and unfairness of this system, its defenders argue that it ordinarily "works" just fine. States award electors based on the outcome of the popular vote in the state. Those electors almost always end up voting the way they're expected to. And the winner of the national popular vote is usually also the winner in the Electoral College.

But "usually" will be cold comfort to Democrats, who have now won the popular vote and lost the Electoral College in two of the past five elections.

What is the Electoral College, and how does it work?

The presidential election is generally portrayed as a battle to win states and their accompanying electoral votes. Hillary Clinton won Vermont, so she got its three electoral votes. Donald Trump won Alaska, so he got its three electoral votes. Whoever gets to 270 or more electoral votes first—a majority of the 538 total—wins the election.

So rather simply trying to win the most *actual votes* in the country, a presidential campaign must try to put together a map of *state victories* that will amass more than 270 electoral votes. That's the simplified version.

What's happening under the hood, though, is more complicated. When people go to the polls to vote for a presidential candidate, what they are actually doing is voting for each party's nominated slate of *electors* in their respective states (or, in the case of Maine and Nebraska, in congressional districts too).

So when Donald Trump won the state of Alaska, the practical effect was that the Republican Party's nominated elector slate there—former Gov. Sean Parnell, Jacqueline Tupou, and Carolyn Leman—officially became Alaska's three electors.

This process repeated itself across the country, resulting in the selection of the Electoral College—the 538 electors who will cast their votes for president in their respective states this Monday. (In the modern era, this ceremonial occasion has been a formality that reiterates an outcome known well in advance.)

But the outcome of the presidential election is really just settled in a few swing states, right?

The Democratic and Republican parties have each developed solid bases in a series of states that are all but certain to vote for them in a presidential year. But the Electoral College winner will be determined by those few swing states that are more divided politically and look like they could go either way. This year, only the states in gray above were decided by a margin of less than 9 percentage points, as of Wednesday afternoon.

The swing states' dominance is a consequence of the fact that almost every state chooses to allot all its electoral votes to whoever comes in first place statewide, regardless of his or her margin of victory.

That is, it doesn't matter whether Clinton wins New York by a 30 percent margin or a 10 percent margin, since she'll get the same amount of electoral votes either way. But the difference between winning Florida by 0.1 percent and losing it by 0.1 percent is crucial, since 29 electoral votes could flip.

Naturally, then, when the general election comes around, candidates ignore every noncompetitive state—meaning the vast majority of the country—and pour their resources into the few that tend to swing back and forth between Republicans and Democrats. That's the best strategy for reaching that magic number, 270.

That seems unfair.

Well, there's a lot that's unfair—or at the very least undemocratic—about the Electoral College.

For one, the winner of the nationwide popular vote can lose the presidency. In 2000, Al Gore won half a million more votes than George W. Bush nationwide, but Bush won the presidency after he was declared the winner in Florida by a mere 537 votes. And that wasn't the first time—electoral college/popular vote splits happened in 1876 and 1888 too, and occurred in 2016 too.

Second, there's swing state privilege. Millions of votes in safe states end up being "wasted," at least in terms of the presidential race, because it makes no difference whether Clinton wins California by 4 million votes, 400,000 votes, or 40 votes—in any scenario, she gets its 55 electors. Meanwhile, states like Florida and Ohio get the power to tip the outcome just because they happen to be closely divided politically.

Third, a small state bias is also built in, since every state is guaranteed at least three electors (the combination of their representation in the House and Senate). The way this shakes out in the math, the 4 percent of the country's population in the smallest states end up being allotted 8 percent of Electoral College votes.

And fourth, there's the possibility for those electors themselves to hijack the outcome.

Wait, the electors can hijack the outcome of the presidential election? What?

For decades, it's been assumed that the 538 electors will essentially rubber-stamp the outcome in their respective states, and they mostly have. But there's scarily little *assurance* that they'll actually do so.

According to the National Conference of State Legislatures, about 30 of the 50 states have passed laws "binding" their electors to vote in accordance with the presidential popular vote in their state. But in most, the penalty for not doing so is only a fine, and it's unclear whether stiffer penalties would hold up in court—it's never been tested, and the Constitution does appear to give the electors the right to make the final call. Furthermore, there are still 20 or so states that haven't even tried to bind their electors.

This hasn't mattered much in the past because, almost always, the parties do a good enough job of vetting their respective electoral slates to ensure that they will indeed loyally back their party's presidential nominee.

But there have been a few rogue, faithless, or just plain incompetent electors over the years—and their votes have all been counted as cast.

- In 1837, rogue electors from Virginia briefly blocked the seating of the vice president-elect because they were offended that he had a mixed-race common-law wife. (The Senate overrode them.)
- A Democratic elector from Tennessee cast his ballot for segregationist third-party candidate Strom Thurmond in 1948, and a Republican elector from North Carolina voted for segregationist third-party candidate George Wallace in 1968.
- In 2000, an elector from Washington, DC, withheld an electoral vote from Al Gore, because she wanted to protest the fact that DC didn't have representation in Congress.

- Perhaps most bizarrely of all, in 2004, an elector from Minnesota who was supposed to vote for John Kerry for president instead voted for *John Edwards*. (It's believed that this was an accident, but since the votes were cast anonymously, we don't really know for sure. Great system!)
- And this year, one Democratic elector candidate from Washington state has repeatedly said that he will "absolutely not" cast his ballot for Hillary Clinton if she wins his state. We'll see whether he follows through.

Rogue electors have never been numerous enough to actually affect the outcome of a presidential race. But it really doesn't look like there's much stopping them should they choose to do so.

Now, some defenders of the system, like Georgetown professor Jason Brennan, take the comforting view that the power of electors to go rogue is a good thing, since they could conceivably save America from a popularly elected majoritarian candidate who could oppress the minority.

But it seems just as likely, if not more likely, that electors could *install* that candidate with dictatorial tendencies *against* that popular will. Perhaps some electors are wise sages with better judgment than the American people, but others are likely malign, corrupt, or driven by their own idiosyncratic beliefs. (You'll notice above that several of those historical rogue electors in history had racist motivations.)

In any case, if we had a process in which the electors were notable citizens who were chosen *because* they're supposed to exercise good judgment, maybe Brennan's defense would make sense. But in the system we have today, the electors are chosen to be rubber stamps. As a result, there's incredibly little attention paid to who those electors even are outside internal party machinations in each state. Any defection by an elector would, essentially, be a random act that could that could hold our system hostage.

Why do we use such a bizarre system anyway?

The electoral college is, essentially, a vestigial structure—a leftover from a bygone era in which the founding fathers specifically *did not* want a nationwide vote of the American people to choose their next president.

Instead, the framers gave a small, lucky group of people called the "electors" the power to make that choice. These would be some upstanding citizens chosen by the various states, who would make up their own minds on who should be the president (they'd have to vote on the same day in their respective home states, to make it tougher for them to coordinate with each other).

The Constitution remained silent on just how these elite electors would be chosen, saying only that each state legislature would decide how to appoint them. Initially, some state legislators picked the electors themselves, while other states had some form of statewide vote in which the electors themselves would be candidates.

But over the new nation's first few decades, two powerful trends in American politics brought attention to the Electoral College system's shortcomings—the rise of national political parties that would contest presidential elections, and the growing consensus that all white men (not just the elite) should get the right to vote, including for president.

The parties and states responded to these trends by trying to jury-rig the existing system. Political parties began to nominate slates of electors in each state—electors they believed could be counted on to vote for the presidential nominee. Eventually, many states even passed laws *requiring* electors to vote for their party's presidential nominee.

Meanwhile, by the 1830s, almost every state had changed its laws so that all electors were chosen winner-take-all through a statewide vote, according to Richard Berg-Andersson. The point of all this was to try to make the presidential election function like ordinary statewide elections for governor or senator, at least within each state.

Well, are there arguments for the Electoral College?

It's tough to argue with a straight face that this bizarre system is *inherently* better than just a simple vote. After all, why doesn't any state elect its governor with an "Electoral College" of various counties? Why does pretty much every other country that elects a president use a simple popular vote, or a vote accompanied with a runoff?

Now, you can argue that the Electoral College's seeming distortions of the popular will aren't as bad as they seem—for instance, by pointing out that swing states tend to swing along with the nation rather than overriding its will, or that the popular vote winner almost always wins. But of course, that's not guaranteed to always be the case, and the biggest major exception (the 2000 election) was an incredibly consequential one.

Others try to fearmonger about the prospect of a contested nationwide recount—which, sure, would be ugly, but if you'll recall, the Florida recount was also extremely ugly. And since there are so many more votes cast nationally, it's much less likely that the national vote would end up a near tie than that a tipping point's state vote would end up as a near tie.

Some argue that the Electoral College ensures regional balance, since it's mathematically impossible for a candidate with overwhelming support from just one region to be elected. But realistically, the country is big and broad enough that this couldn't happen under a popular vote system either—any regional candidate would need to get *some* support outside his or her region.

But when we get down to brass tacks, the most serious objections to reforming the Electoral College come from rural and small-state elites who fear that under a national popular vote system, they'd be ignored and elections would be decided by people who live in cities.

Gary Gregg of the University of Louisville wrote in 2012 that eliminating the Electoral College would lead to "dire consequences." Specifically, he feared that elections would "strongly tilt" in favor of "candidates who can win huge electoral margins in the country's major metropolitan areas." He continued:

> If the United States does away with the Electoral College, future presidential elections will go to candidates and parties willing to cater to urban voters and skew the nation's policies toward big-city interests. Small-town issues and rural values will no longer be their concern.

And Pete du Pont, a former governor of Delaware (three electoral votes), has made a similar case, calling proposals for a national popular vote an "urban power grab."

But a national popular vote system wouldn't *devalue* the votes of people who live in rural states and small towns. It would *accurately* value them by treating them equal to people who live in cities, rather than giving them an extra weighting. Furthermore, small-state interests are built into the Senate's math (where Delaware absurdly gets as many senators as California), and many House districts are rural. So rural and small-state areas are hardly hurting for national political representation.

Sure, candidates might end up spending less time stumping in the rural areas that currently happen to be lucky enough to fall within the borders of swing states, and more time in urban centers. But is that really a convincing rebuttal to the pretty basic and obvious argument that in the most important electoral choice Americans make, their votes should be treated equally?

Is there any hope that the US will ditch the Electoral College someday?

For decades, polls have shown that large majorities of Americans would prefer a popular vote system instead of the Electoral College. For instance, a 2013 Gallup poll showed 63 percent of adults wanted to do away with it, and a mere 29 percent wanted to keep it. (However, these margins have tightened since the 2016 election.)

But to ditch the Electoral College entirely, the US would have to pass a constitutional amendment (passed by two-thirds of the House and Senate and approved by 38 states)—or convene a constitutional convention (which has never been done, but would have to be called for by 34 states). Either method is vanishingly unlikely, because each would require many small states to approve a change that would reduce their influence on the presidential outcome.

There is one potential workaround, however: the National Popular Vote Interstate Compact, a clever proposal that uses the Constitution's ambiguity on electors to its own ends.

A state signing on to the compact agrees that it will pledge all its electors not to its state winner but to the victor in the *national* popular vote—*but only if* states controlling 270 or more electoral votes have agreed to do the same. If they do, and everything works as planned, then whoever wins the popular vote will necessarily win the electoral vote too.

It's a fun proposal that's already been enacted into law by 10 states (including massive California and New York) and the District of Columbia, which together control 165 electoral votes. But there's one big obstacle: All of the states that have adopted it are solidly Democratic, with zero being Republican or swing states.

So unless a bunch of swing states decide to reduce their own power, or Republican politicians conclude that a system bringing the power of small and rural states in line with that of big urban centers is a good idea, the compact isn't going to get the support it needs, as Nate Silver has written. (Furthermore, it wouldn't solve the rogue elector problem.)

As messed up as the Electoral College is, then, we're likely stuck with it for some time. Your safe state vote might be wasted, or it might even be subverted by rogue electors.

But at least you'll get to draw fun maps.

Periodical and Internet Sources Bibliography

The following articles have been selected to supplement the diverse views presented in this chapter.

Akhil Reed Amar, "The Troubling Reason the Electoral College Exists, *Time*, November 10, 2016.

Adam Gopnik, "We Could Have Been Canada: Was the American Revolution Such a Good Idea?" *New Yorker*, May 15, 2017. http://www.newyorker.com/magazine/2017/05/15/we-could-have-been-canada?currentPage=all&wpisrc=nl_daily202&wpmm=1.

Kent Greenfield, "If Corporations Are People, They Should Act Like It," *Atlantic*, February 1, 2015. https://www.theatlantic.com/politics/archive/2015/02/if-corporations-are-people-they-should-act-like-it/385034.

Adam Liptak, "Smaller States Find Outsize Clout Growing in Senate." *New York Times*, March 10, 2013. http://www.nytimes.com/interactive/2013/03/11/us/politics/democracy-tested.html.

Andrew A. Michta, "The Deconstruction of the West," *American Interest*, April 12, 2017. https://www.the-american-interest.com/2017/04/12/the-deconstruction-of-the-west.

Ruth Patrick. "How Poverty Makes People Less Likely to Vote," *Guardian*, May 16, 2017. https://www.theguardian.com/society/2017/may/16/poverty-election-vote-apathy.

Hans A. von Spakvoksy, "Does 'One Person, One Vote' Really Mean What It Says?" Heritage Foundation, August 3, 2015. http://www.heritage.org/election-integrity/commentary/does-one-person-one-vote-really-mean-what-it-says.

Nina Totenberg, "When Did Companies Become People? Excavating the Legal Evoluation," NPR, July 18, 2014. http://www.npr.org/2014/07/28/335288388/when-did-companies-become-people-excavating-the-legal-evolution.

Chapter 4

What Does the Future Hold for Western Democracy?

Chapter Preface

When Benjamin Franklin responded to the citizen who met him as he exited the Constitutional Convention, he seemed to warn her that the new republic would be fragile. As we have seen in the previous chapters, Franklin was right to be concerned; democracy is not something to be taken for granted. A robust democracy requires a great deal of work and vigilance on the part of its citizens, and for a variety of reasons democracy in the West is going through a difficult period. As far as we know, Franklin did not on that Autumn afternoon offer the woman any suggestions for what the citizens might do to "keep" that republic. But people have been giving the matter thought ever since. The authors of the viewpoints in this last chapter take up that question. They are interested in matters that concern the future of Western democracy. And those are necessarily issues that concern young people. How millennials view their government, the future of NATO, the rise of fake and biased news, and the importance of education—and what type of education might be most useful—are all topics that are discussed in the viewpoints you will read here.

Many serious concerns have been raised in this volume—but there is much hope as well. Democracy may be fragile, but the citizens of Western Democracies are a robust group, and for the most part they care more deeply about their rights and freedoms than it sometimes seems. The very fact that so many articles and blog posts have been written about this issue indicates that many thoughtful people are thinking and considering what to do to protect this old yet vulnerable form of government. As Winston Churchill once put it, "… it has been said that democracy is the worst form of Government except for all those other forms that have been tried from time to time." Protecting it might be difficult, but is probably worth the effort.

Viewpoint 1

> *"As a group college graduates contribute more and take less from society."*

Democracies Are Healthier with Educated Citizens

Cindy Miller

In the following viewpoint, Cindy Miller argues that an educated populace is essential to a smoothly running democracy. The author begins by discussing the more oft-mentioned benefits of postsecondary education to society at large, such as the creation of more working citizens to pay taxes, and then points out that the value of an education goes beyond providing the skills and training necessary to get a job. Educated citizens, she says, are more likely to be involved in community service programs and engage in civic participation. They are less likely to be dogmatic and ethnocentric. Miller is the director of the Kansas City campus of Columbia College.

As you read, consider the following questions:

1. What sorts of programs does this author say are the kinds of education that are beneficial to a society?
2. How do children benefit from having educated parents?
3. Does this author say that people with post-secondary education are more likely to vote?

"An Educated Society is a Stronger Society," by Cindy Miller, The EvoLLLution, November 18, 2013. Reprinted by permission.

In early 2009 President Obama proclaimed that "every American will need to get more than a high school diploma" and that "America cannot lead in the 21st century unless we have the best educated, most competitive workforce in the world."

Not an easy task.

President Obama and the Department of Education are not merely referring to bachelor's degrees and beyond, but also to associate's degrees, short-term certificate programs and workforce training.

Several pundits have predicted that, in a few short years, as much as two-thirds of the new jobs available in the United States will require some form of postsecondary education. Much of the growth is expected in the fields of health care, science, technology and education.

Beyond the need for workers to fill specific jobs, there are grander reasons to encourage people to pursue postsecondary education. The personal benefits are fairly obvious – research has shown over and over again that a college education leads to higher income earnings over one's lifetime. College attendance also has been shown to improve health and life expectancy and helps develop a network of people who enrich one's personal and professional life.

What about the benefits to the community and society as a whole? Bottom line, as a group college graduates contribute more and take less from society.

Increased income means higher income taxes paid by college graduates to support the community, state and country. Less is spent on unemployment compensation, welfare and other social programs when there are more college graduates. In fact, some estimates of savings in these areas run from $800 to $2,000 for each college graduate when compared to a high school graduate.

There is a greater chance that degree recipients have full-time jobs that provide health insurance and retirement benefits. In addition, college graduates are less likely to be incarcerated. For every four high school graduates jailed, only one college graduate is jailed, saving taxpayers an average per-prisoner cost of more than $20,000 per year.

Children are better off if their parents graduate from college. These parents are more involved with their children's education in and outside of school. Their preschool children have a higher likelihood of being read to, and are more likely to be able to count to 20 and write their name. Children of college graduates are more inclined to attend college themselves.

College graduates are more involved in community service programs and civic participation. A greater percentage of college grads compared to non-grads are active in some form of political process. More college degree recipients read local newspapers and as a consequence have greater awareness and understanding of community, regional and national issues. This leads them to vote in greater numbers. After all, as the President and countless philosophers and political scientists have noted in the past, a healthy democracy relies on an educated populace.

College graduates are more critically thinking, and display more creative attributes due to the complex intellectual and academic skills they learned through their postsecondary studies. Graduates are more independent, and have fewer tendencies toward dogmatism and ethnocentrism. They are better able to work collaboratively in diverse environments.

Other societal benefits come from robust collegiate institutions that enhance economic development through innovative research programs and partnerships with business and/or government entities.

If you stopped a college graduate on the street and asked why he/she went to college, the answer would probably be "to get a good job." However, colleges and universities know a very important function of education is to not only train workers, but to produce an engaged citizenry. The value of growing intellectual capital and cultivating a sense of social responsibility to the local and global community cannot be reduced to mere dollars and cents.

Viewpoint 2

> *"Higher education institutions do decently with knowledge transmission. Unfortunately, they do dismally transmitting skills."*

To Be Successful, You Need More Than Knowledge

Michael Schrage

In the following viewpoint, Michael Schrage makes the case for the resurgence of a different kind of education. The author goes so far to say that a college education is not only unnecessary, but that in many cases hinders success. Contrary to the previous viewpoint, in which its author contends that democracies are stronger when the population is educated (specifically, college educated), Schrage argues that skill is far more important than education, even in fields where a college degree is required. Schrage is a fellow with the Sloan School of Management at the Massachusetts Institute of Technology (MIT).

"Higher Education Is Overrated," by Michael Schrage, Harvard Business School Publishing, July 29, 2010. Reprinted by permission.

As you read, consider the following questions:

1. How, according to Schrage, might a degree from an elite educational establishment be worth less than it seems?
2. What examples does he use to show that a college degree is not necessary for successful entrepreneurship?
3. According to this viewpoint, why do people get hired and paid well?

With innovation, entrepreneurship and significantly smarter fiscal policies, America should eventually escape its "hireless recovery." But what won't hasten new hiring—and might even dampen job prospects—is the mythical belief that higher education invariably leads to higher employment and better jobs. It doesn't. Foolish *New York Times* stories notwithstanding, education is a misleading-to-malignant proxy for economic productivity or performance. Knowledge may be power, but "knowledge from college" is neither predictor nor guarantor of success. Growing numbers of informed observers increasingly describe a higher education "bubble" that makes a college and/or university education a subprime investment for too many attendees.

Are they right? I don't know. But painfully clear to many employers are serious gaps between elite educational credentials and actual individual competence. College transcripts spackled with As and Bs—particularly from liberal arts and humanities programs—reveal less about a candidate's capabilities than most serious employers need to know. Even top-tier MBA degrees often say more about the desire to have an important credential than about any greater capacity to be a good leader or manager. The curricular formalities of higher education—as opposed to its informal networks of friends and connections—may be less valuable now than they were a decade ago. In other words, alumni networks may be more economically valuable than whatever one studied in class. "Where you went" may prove professionally more helpful than "what you know." That certainly undermines "value of education" arguments. While higher education itself isn't marginal or unimportant, its actual market impact on employment prospects may be wildly misunderstood. In "Econ 101" terms for job-hunters: time spent cultivating your Facebook/Linked-In network(s) may be a better investment than taking that Finance elective.

Eduzealots have done a truly awful thing to serious human capital conversations and analyses around employment. By vociferously championing higher education as key to economic success, they've distorted important public policy debates about how and why people get hired and paid well. They've undermined useful arguments about "street smarts" versus "book smarts." Treating education as the best proxy for human capital is like using patents as your proxy for measuring innovation—its underlying logic shouldn't obscure the fact that you'll underweigh market leaders like WalMart, Google, Tata and Toyota. Dare I point out that Microsoft's Bill Gates, Dell's Michael Dell, Apple's Steve Jobs, Oracle's Larry Ellison and Facebook's Mark Zuckerberg are all college drop-outs? The point isn't to declare a college degree antithetical to launching a high-tech juggernaut but to observe that, perhaps, higher education isn't essential to effective entrepreneurship.

We have a huge branding issue. Pundits and policy-makers jabber about the need to educate people to compete in knowledge-intensive industries. But knowledge doesn't represent even half the intensity of this industrial challenge. What really matters are skills. The grievously undervalued human capital issue here isn't quality education in school but quality of skills in markets. Establishing correlations, let alone causality, between them is hard. (Michael Polanyi's classic "Personal Knowledge" brilliantly articulates this.) A computer science PhD doesn't make one a good programmer. There is a world of difference between getting an "A" in robotics class and winning a "bot" competition. MIT's motto isn't *Mens et Manus* (Latin for Mind and Hand) by accident. Great knowledge is not the same as great skill. Worse yet, decent knowledge doesn't guarantee even decent skills. Unfortunately, educrats and eduzealots behave as if college English degrees mean their recipients can write and that philosophy degrees mean their holders can rigorously think. That's not true. Feel free to comment below if you disagree....

As Atkinson's anecdotes affirm, there's no shortage of "well-educated" college graduates who can't write intelligible synopses or manage simple spreadsheets. I know doctoral candidates in statistics and operations research who find adapting their superb technical expertise to messy, real-world problem solving extraordinarily difficult. Their great knowledge doesn't confer great skill. Nevertheless, you would find their research and their resumes impressive. You should. But focusing on their formal educational accomplishments misrepresents their skill set outside the academy. Academic and classroom markets are profoundly different than business and workplace markets. Why should anyone be surprised that serious knowledge/skill gaps dominate those differences?

Higher education institutions do decently with knowledge transmission. Unfortunately, they do dismally transmitting skills. Pun intended, that's—apparently—not their job. That's also why "human capital" debates and investment policies going forward should weight skills over knowledge. When I look at who is getting hired, purported knowledge almost always matters less than demonstrable skills. The distinctions aren't subtle; they're immense. How do they manifest themselves? These hires don't have resumes highlighting educational pedigrees and accomplishments; their resumes emphasize their skill sets. Instead of listing aspirations and achievements, these resumes present portfolios around performance. They link to blogs, published articles, PowerPoint presentations, podcasts and webinars the candidates produced. The traditional two-page resume has been turned into a "personal productivity portal" that empowers prospective employers to quite literally interact with their candidate's work.

Unsurprisingly, this simultaneously complements and reinforces the employer-side due diligence that's emerged during this recession: firms have both the luxury and necessity to find the best possible candidates for open positions. Yes, they're looking for appropriate levels of educational accomplishment but, really, what they most want are people who have the skills they need. More importantly, they want to actually see those skills—be they written, computed, designed and/or presented. Professional services firms I know now don't hesitate to ask a serious candidate to demonstrate their sincerity and skills by asking them to show how they might "adapt" a presentation for one of the company's own clients. Verbal fluency and presence impresses headhunters and interviewers. But the ability to virtually demonstrate one's professional skills increasingly matters more.

This is part of the vast structural shift in the human capital marketplace worldwide. Firms have the ability and incentive to be far more selective in their hires. But project managers and professionals also have the bandwidth and desire to showcase their skills. The resume is rapidly mutating away from a documentary string of alphanumeric text into a multimedia platform that projects precisely the brand image and substance a job candidate seeks to convey. Did they teach you that in college or grad school? Of course not. Will you learn that by hanging around LinkedIn or Facebook? Probably not.

Is this how human capital markets will become more efficient and effective tomorrow? Absolutely. You've got to have skill to show off your knowledge.

Viewpoint 3

> *"Let's be clear: presidents, prime ministers, their administrations as well as their political adversaries all cherry-pick facts to embarrass their opponents."*

The Media Does Not Make up Fake News, but It Does Have Biases

Eric R. Mandel

In the following viewpoint, Eric R. Mandel addresses the role of the free press in democratic societies. Several of the previous viewpoints have stressed the importance to democracy of an educated and informed public. US president Donald Trump often says or tweets that the media is making up the news. Mandel doesn't believe that the media makes up the news, but believes the problem is that the media in the United States is not as unbiased as it should be. He is particularly bothered by the intrusion of opinion into the reporting of facts. Mandel is the director of MEPIN and frequent contributor to the Jerusalem Post.

"An Activist Media, Fake News, Editorialized Stories and Democracy," by Mepin, Mepin, March 16, 2017. Reprinted by permission.

As you read, consider the following questions:

1. What does Mandel mean by an "agenda driven" media?
2. According to this viewpoint, what is the essential role of media in a democracy?
3. After reading this viewpoint, does it seem as if this author has an agenda?

If I were to counsel Trump, I would tell him to stop claiming that the media is making up the news, but explain to the public that his beef with news organizations is their slanted reporting.

A few years ago, I asked an editorial writer at *Haaretz* if he was troubled by accusations that his paper editorialized news stories to fit its agenda. His response was, "If you don't like it, read another paper."

A recent *New York Times* front page news story on media bias read, "Biased? Probably. Oppositional? Maybe. Essential? In theory, but the enemy? Not so much." It should be no surprise to any informed consumer of news that media outlets practice activist journalism, commingling opinion and fact.

Most of the uproar regarding media bias is in response to the attacks by US President Donald Trump on an activist media. The president has referred to editorialized news as "fake news," the media as the "opposition party" and the press as the "enemy of the American people."

None of this is healthy for any democratic political system. Presidential or executive credibility is essential for a functioning democracy, and this type of rhetoric can undermine the public trust.

Transparency is essential for the media's role as a watchdog for a democracy's citizenry, but an agenda-driven media in both Israel and the United States perpetrates a fraud on the public.

An activist, agenda-driven press, or editorialized news passed off as straight news, deserves condemnation, but Trump's calling it "fake" confuses the public, some of whom, especially those who already don't like him much, will think he is denying facts.

Let's be clear: presidents, prime ministers, their administrations as well as their political adversaries all cherry-pick facts to embarrass their opponents. But this has gotten much worse in both Israel and America.

Activist media assertions have been front and center in the US regarding many issues, none more contentious than the Israeli-Palestinian conflict. Organizations like CAMERA, Palestinian Media Watch (PMW), NGO Monitor, MEMRI, Accuracy in Media and Honest Reporting have been created to make the public aware that many mainstream news organizations too often present facts out of context to advance what they consider a politically correct agenda.

Contempt and lack of civil respect for contrary opinions oozes from the columns and editorials of the *New York Times*, with far too many ad hominem attacks. The Times created its ombudsman position in part in response to cancellations of subscriptions due to its anti-Israel bias, disproportionately focusing on alleged Israeli transgressions while ignoring far more egregious stories in the Middle East and the world.

So which is more dangerous, editorialized news that is technically correct in some sense but is meant to fool the public, or truly fake news that has no or little factual content? Sometimes the bias is insidious, as in article placement, censorship by omission of information that contradicts an agenda, burying a countervailing viewpoint at the end of the piece where few readers will venture, or choosing someone who sounds not worthy of respect to present the opposing side.

I have interviewed some leading editors who have told me that if you are perceived to have a view not matching the agenda of the media outlet, you will be marginalized.

The press's prejudice and influence is not just in the international arena, but has infected even the American judicial system.

Judge Lawrence Silverman, a senior judge on the US Circuit Court of Appeals, wrote in *The Wall Street Journal* that "the press's orientation is sympathetic to activist results, which I think it is safe to say are largely on the left," causing some justices not to be blind in rendering a decision.

A Supreme Court influenced by an activist press—is that good for democracy?

Which brings us back to fake news. Does the American or Israeli press present false news? The answer, overwhelmingly, is no. If they did, it would be much easier to deal with, as illegitimate facts are much easier to discredit than opinionated news bias cleverly concealed by biased journalists.

No Israeli prime minister or American president has ever had easy dealings with the press. That is why Trump's charges of fake news remain credible to many of his supporters. If I were to council Trump, I would tell him to stop claiming that the media is making up the news, but explain to the public that his beef with news organizations is their slanted reporting.

There is no doubt that president Barack Obama received much less scrutiny than either president George W. Bush or Trump because of the media's affinity for Obama's agenda, but the Trump administration needs to have a tougher skin when it comes under legitimate criticism for policy differences.

Israeli media is less apologetic in its bias. At a meeting I had with a leading Israeli journalist a couple of years ago she referred to her paper as the anti-Netanyahu paper.

Donald Trump and Prime Minister Benjamin Netanyahu will be in the history books in a few years, but the biased media will still be with us.

The lesson for the American and Israeli people to learn is that an independent press is vital to their democracies, even when it presents uncomfortable truths. But they need to wake up and realize that their news sources are far too biased, and that they need to demand an end to editorialized news, as well as an end to demonization of the press.

"No civilization can tolerate a fixed expectation of dishonest communications without falling apart from a breakdown in mutual trust."

The Death of Honesty Could Mean the Death of Democracy

William Damon

In the following viewpoint, William Damon begins by discussing the value of honesty and its importance to a civilized society. Though honesty is not a virtue in every situation, according to Damon, a civilized society cannot exist without the expectation that most members will be honest most of the time. More importantly, the author says that honesty is essential for self government. Damon is a senior fellow at the Hoover Institution, the director of the Stanford Center on Adolescence, and a professor of education at Stanford University.

As you read, consider the following questions:

1. Is honesty not always a moral value? In what circumstances is lying a greater virtue than truth, according to Damon?
2. Why, according to this viewpoint, is it so important for members of a society to be able to expect a certain degree in honesty in one another?
3. Why is teaching and demanding honesty in school so important to a democracy?

For a number of reasons, people do not always stick to the truth when they speak. Some of the reasons are justifiable—for example, humane considerations such as tact and the avoidance of greater harm. Reassuring an ungainly teenager that he or she looks great may be a kind embroidery of the truth. In a more consequential instance, misinforming storm troopers about the whereabouts of a hidden family during the Nazi occupation of Europe was an honorable and courageous deception.

Honesty is not a wholly detached moral virtue demanding strict allegiance at all times. Compassion, diplomacy, and life-threatening circumstances sometimes require a departure from the entire unadulterated truth. Some vocations seem to demand occasional deception for success or survival. Politicians, for example, are especially hard-pressed to tell the truth consistently. Perhaps this is because, as George Orwell once observed, the very function of political speech is to hide, soften, or misrepresent difficult truths. Orwell was clearly skeptical about any expectation to the contrary. In "Politics and the English Language," he put it this way: "Political language—and with variations this is true of all political parties, from Conservatives to Anarchists—is designed to make lies sound truthful and murder respectable, and to give an appearance of solidity to pure wind."

Although in this case Orwell himself may have been guilty of overstatement for purposes of rhetorical effect, his claim cannot be totally dismissed. It would be naïve (or cynical) for anyone in today's world to act shocked whenever a politician tries to hide the real truth from the public. For ordinary citizens, keeping up with the daily news means a constant process of speculating about what the politicians really meant by what they said and what they actually believe. It certainly does not mean taking what any of them say at face value.

Yet to recognize that honesty is not an absolute standard demanded for every life circumstance—and that we can expect a certain amount of deceit from even our respected public figures—is not to say that the virtue of honesty can be disregarded with impunity. A basic intent to be truthful, along with an assumption that people can be generally taken at their word, is required for all sustained civilized dealings.

Teaching honesty is no longer a priority in our schools.

No civilization can tolerate a fixed expectation of dishonest communications without falling apart from a breakdown in mutual trust. All human relations rely upon confidence that those in the relations will, as a rule, tell the truth. Honesty builds and solidifies a relationship with trust; and too many breaches in honesty can corrode relations beyond repair. Friendships, family, work, and civic relations all suffer whenever dishonesty comes to light. The main reason that no one wants to be known as a liar is that people shun liars because they can't be trusted.

Honesty's vital role in human society has been observed and celebrated for all of recorded history. The Romans considered the goddess *Veritas* to be the "mother of virtue"; Confucius considered honesty to be the essential source of love, communication, and fairness between people; and of course, the Bible's Old Testament prohibited bearing false witness. It is also noteworthy that the two most universally heralded U. S. presidents (George Washington, who "could not tell a lie," and Abraham Lincoln, who was known as "Honest Abe") were widely acclaimed for their trustworthiness.

In a similar vein, religious leader Gordon Hinckley has written that, "where there is honesty, other virtues will follow"—indicating, as did the Romans, the pivotal role of truthfulness in all moral behavior and development. Hinckley's comment was made in the context of his alarm-sounding book on "neglected virtues," and it points to the problematic status of honesty in our society today. Although truthfulness is essential for good human relationships and personal integrity, it is often abandoned in pursuit of other life priorities.

Indeed, there may be a perception in many key areas of contemporary life—law, business, politics, among others—that expecting honesty on a regular basis is a naïve and foolish attitude, a "loser's" way of operating. Such a perception is practically a mandate for personal dishonesty and a concession to interpersonal distrust. When we no longer assume that those who communicate with us are at least trying to tell the truth, we give up on them as trustworthy persons and deal with them only in a strictly instrumental manner. The bounds of mutual moral obligation dissolve, and the laws of the jungle reemerge.

Our serious problem today is not simply that many people routinely tell lies. As I have noted, people have departed from the truth for one reason or another all throughout human history. The problem now is that we seem to be reaching a dysfunctional tipping point in which an essential commitment to truthfulness no longer seems to be assumed in our society. If this is indeed the case, the danger is that the bonds of trust important in any society, and essential for a free and democratic one, will dissolve so that the kinds of discourse required to self-govern will become impossible.

A basic intent to be truthful is required for all sustained civilized dealings.

What are the signs of this in contemporary society? In professional and business circles, a now-familiar complaint is, "It used to be your word was good, but those days are gone." In print, broadcast, and online news coverage, journalism has lost credibility with much of the public for its perceived biases in representing the facts. In civic affairs, political discourse is no longer considered to be a source of genuine information. Rather, it is assumed that leaders make statements merely to posture for effect, and not to engage in discussion or debate. In such an environment, facts may be manipulated or made up in service of a predetermined interest, not presented accurately and then examined in good faith. This is troubling, because civic leaders set the tone for communications throughout the public sphere.

Most troubling of all is that honesty is no longer a priority in many of the settings where young people are educated. The future of every society depends upon the character development of its young. It is in the early years of life—the first two decades especially—when basic virtues that shape character are acquired. Although people can learn, grow, and reform themselves at any age, this kind of learning becomes increasingly difficult as habits solidify over time. Honesty is a prime example of a virtue that becomes habitual over the years if practiced consistently—and the same can be said about dishonesty.

Honesty is the character virtue most closely linked to every school's academic mission. In matters of "academic integrity," which generally revolve around cheating, schools have a primary responsibility to convey to students the importance of honesty as a practical and ethical virtue. Unfortunately, many of our schools today are failing this responsibility.

Of all the breeches that can tear deeply into the moral fabric of a school, cheating is among the most damaging, because it throws in doubt the school's allegiance to truth and fairness. Cheating in school is unethical for at least four reasons: 1) it gives students who cheat an unfair advantage over those who do not cheat; 2) it is an act of dishonesty in a setting dedicated to a quest for truthful knowledge, 3) it is a violation of trust between student and teacher; and 4) it disrespects the code of conduct and the social order of the school. As such, one would expect that cheating would provide educators with an ideal platform for imparting the key moral standards of honesty, integrity, trust, and fairness.

Incredibly, some teachers have actually encouraged students to cheat.

For educators looking for opportunities to help students learn from their mistakes, there is plenty of material to work with: research has shown that almost three-quarters of American college students (that is, students who have made it through high school) admit to having cheated at least once in their pre-college academic work. Donald McCabe, the most prominent contemporary researcher on school cheating, has concluded that "Cheating is prevalent, and…some forms of cheating have increased dramatically in the last 30 years."

Yet many teachers, in order to avoid legal action and other contention, look the other way if their students copy test answers or hand in plagiarized papers. Some teachers excuse students because they believe that "sharing" schoolwork is motivated by loyalty to friends. Some teachers sympathize with student cheaters because they consider the tests that students take to be flawed, unfair, or too difficult. Such sympathy can be taken to extremes, as in the case of one teacher, observed by an educational writer, who held that "it was the teacher who was immoral for having given the students such a burdensome assignment..." when a group of students was caught cheating.

Incredibly, some teachers actually have encouraged students to cheat; and some have even cheated themselves when reporting student test scores. In July 2011, a widely-reported cheating scandal erupted in school systems in and around Atlanta, Georgia. State investigators found a pattern of "organized and systemic misconduct" dating back for over ten years. One-hundred-and-seventy-eight teachers, and the principals of half of the system's schools, aided and abetted students who were cheating on their tests. Top administrators ignored news reports of this cheating: a *New York Times* story described "a culture of fear and intimidation that prevented many teachers from speaking out."

Nor was this an isolated incident. In a feature on school testing, CBS News reported the following: "New York education officials found 21 proven cases of teacher cheating. Teachers have read off answers during a test, sent students back to correct wrong answers, photocopied secure tests for use in class, inflated scores, and peeked at questions then drilled those topics in class before the test."

With such prominent and recent instances of cheating among students and teachers today, one would expect a concerted effort to articulate and promote the value of honesty in our schools. Yet school programs regarding academic integrity consist of little more than a patchwork of vaguely-stated prohibitions and half-hearted responses. Our schools vacillate between routine neglect and a circle-the wagons reaction if the problem boils over into a public media scandal. There is little consistency, coherence, or transparency in many school policies.

It is practically impossible to find a school that treats academic integrity as a moral issue by employing revealed incidents of cheating to communicate to its student body values such as honesty, respect for rules, and trust. In my own observations, I have noticed a palpable lack of interest among teachers and staff in discussing the moral significance of cheating with students. The problem here is the low priority of honesty in our agenda for schooling specifically and child-rearing in general.

In former days, there was not much hesitancy in our society about using a moral language to teach children essential virtues such as honesty. For us today, it can be a culture shock to leaf through old editions of the McGuffey Readers, used in most American schools until the mid-twentieth century, to see how readily educators once dispensed unambiguous moral lessons to students. Nowadays, when cheating is considered by some teachers to be an excusable response to a difficult assignment, or even a form of pro-social activity, our society risks a future of moral numbness brought on by a decline of honesty and all the virtues that rely on it. As the Founders of our republic warned, the failure to cultivate virtue in citizens can be a lethal threat to any democracy.

> *"The effort to advance democracy is being led not by the West but by the global democracy movement"*

Weakness of Democracy in the West Weakens Democratic Progress Worldwide

Carl Gershman

In the following viewpoint, Carl Gershman argues that many countries are "backsliding" when it comes to democracy, and at least some of the reason for that is the 2008 economic crisis in the West, that slowed globalization. He explains how authoritarian regimes resist democratic movements, and use election interference, the media, and propaganda to reassert control. The author ends on a cautiously optimistic note, pointing out activists are working hard in many nations to work for democracy and individual rights, and that people in Western democracies can take inspiration from them to reassert their own rights and freedoms. Gershman is president of the National Endowment for Democracy.

"Western Paralysis and Retreat Threatens Democratic Progress," by Carl Gershman, World Affairs Journal, May 17, 2016. www.worldaffairsjournal.org; Online Feature. Reprinted with Permission of the World Affairs Institute.

As you read, consider the following questions:

1. What are some of the reasons given by this author for the failure of the Arab Spring?
2. What role is the West playing, according to Gorshman, for the breakdown of democracy in other parts of the world?
3. What is the "moral and political crisis" in the West, as described here?

Democracy is being challenged today as never before since the end of the Cold War. Freedom House has recorded ten consecutive years during which democracy and human rights have declined in more countries than it has advanced. There have been setbacks and backsliding in countries as diverse as Thailand, Venezuela, Hungary, Turkey, Azerbaijan, Bangladesh, and of course in Russia and China as well.

Certainly one of the reasons for the perception that democracy is in decline is the failure of the Arab Spring. Five years ago, in the immediate aftermath of the fall of Egyptian President Hosni Mubarak, there was hope that what was called the Arab Spring might translate into democratic gains in the one region that had been by-passed by the third wave of democratization two decades earlier. But as we know, the Arab Spring quickly turned into an Arab Winter.

In Egypt, there was blame to go around—from the military and the deeply entrenched state bureaucracy that never had any intention of allowing a real transition, to the over-reaching and illiberal Islamists, the fractious secular parties, and civil society groups that were unable to make the transition from street protest to meaningful political action. None of these participants appreciated the need to build consensus on core constitutional principles and democratic reforms, and so, instead of finding a way to build coalitions to move forward, the process descended into a zero-sum struggle for power.

With the exception of Tunisia and Morocco, the failure occurred across the region. A recent report in *The Economist* described the Middle East today as "more benighted than ever." Sisi's regime in Egypt is now more repressive than Mubarak's; state institutions have collapsed in Iraq, Syria, Libya, and Yemen; there is growing sectarian violence fed by the regional contest between Iran and Saudi Arabia; and of course there is the rise of ISIS and international terrorism, which has not only undermined hopes for democratic change in the Middle East, but has given autocrats in the region and beyond a new argument to justify strong-arm rule. It has also led many in the West to conclude—wrongly, in my view—that efforts to advance democracy in the Middle East will encourage instability and harm Western security interests in the region.

Perhaps most troubling has been the geopolitical retreat of the West that has opened the way to the emergence of ISIS and other dangerous developments, among them Iran's expanding influence in the Arab world, Putin's annexation of Crimea and invasion of eastern Ukraine and his reassertion of Russian power in the Middle East for the first time since Sadat cut Egypt's military ties with the Soviet Union after the 1973 war, and not least, China's brazen assertion of power in the South China Sea.

The effect on democracy of the deteriorating geopolitical context has been worsened by a pervasive moral and political crisis in the West. The crisis is partly the result of an extended period of economic stagnation that was triggered by the global financial crisis of 2008 but is rooted in systemic problems, among them increasing indebtedness and large budget deficits, uncontrolled entitlement spending, and growing inequality. There is also a crisis of political dysfunction, exemplified in the United States by political polarization and declining trust in government, and by the rise here and in Europe of a new populism that exploits grievance, fear, and frustration. These developments have undermined democracy's standing and credibility internationally and have emboldened the opponents of liberal democracy, who are rushing to fill the vacuums created by Western paralysis and retreat.

The growing projection of hard power by Russia, China, and Iran, and the increased threat of terrorism, have obscured an equally important expansion of authoritarian soft power in the areas of information, communications technology, ideas, and culture where the advanced democracies had been thought to have had a natural advantage.

Globalization was always considered to be a favorable context for the expansion of democracy and liberal values. Indeed, it was assumed in the aftermath of the Cold War that the West could encourage the liberalization of countries like Russia and China by engaging them and integrating them into the liberal international order. Many believed that the attractions of our culture and life-style, and the impact of the global economy, would inevitably open up autocratic systems.

But it hasn't worked out that way. Against all expectations, these authoritarian countries have not liberalized but have grown more repressive, and far from being changed by efforts to integrate them into the liberal world order, they are subverting and destroying that order to advance their own interests and anti-democratic values.

At the National Endowment for Democracy (NED) we have called this phenomenon "resurgent authoritarianism" and have just come out with a book of essays on the subject called *Authoritarianism Goes Global.* It explains how a number of autocracies—in particular Russia, China, and Iran—have developed new tools and strategies in a number of areas to contain the spread of democracy and to challenge the democracy agenda on different fronts in the "soft power" battle of ideas.

One of these fronts is civil society. Over the last four years, 120 laws that repress and control civil society have been passed in sixty countries—a remarkable commonality over an immensely broad international spectrum. These are laws that seek to frustrate, undermine, and prohibit the activities of democratic civil society groups and individual activists, who are often labeled "foreign agents" and a "fifth column." Russia last year declared NED, the Open Society Foundations, the National Democratic Institute and other organizations "undesirable" and have threatened NGOs that receive support from such international organizations with severe legal penalties. A new law in China puts foreign and local NGOs under the control of the Public Security Bureau, meaning that they are being treated as a security risk.

The goal here is to preemptively block what the autocrats call "colored revolutions," which are popular uprisings like the Orange Revolution in Ukraine, the Velvet Revolution in Czechoslovakia, the Rose Revolution in Georgia, and the Green Revolution in Iran. They hope to do this by cutting civil society groups off from international assistance and placing them under very tight political control.

Information and media are a second front in this battle. As Anne Applebaum and Edward Lucas have noted, autocrats seek to exploit the declining influence of major Western media outlets and the proliferation of online information that makes it harder for people to judge accuracy of news. Russia, China, and Iran are investing heavily in the production of alternative models—RT and Sputnik in the case of Russia, along with a huge range of online vehicles that include "news" websites, information portals, trolls. China has expanded the international reach through its Xinhua state news agency, China Central TV (CCTV), and Confucius Institutes. For its part, Iran is expanding its broadcasting in Spanish over HispanTV, in English over PressTV, and in French, Arabic, Urdu and other languages over its Sahar network.

Peter Pomerantsev has described the Russian propaganda effort as "the weaponization of information." Instead of trying to promote the regime's political line, which was the purpose of Soviet propaganda during the Cold War, its goal now is to undermine the institutions of the West by destroying the credibility of all information. According to Applebaum and Lucas, the Russians encourage cynicism, fear and distrust by spreading scare stories about immigrants and portraying the West as racist and xenophobic. They push the notion that 9/11 was an inside job, that the Zika virus was created by the CIA, and that a German woman had been raped by a Muslim refugee—a phony story that blew up into a scandal and forced Chancellor Angela Merkel to ask German intelligence to investigate the nature and scope of Russian propaganda. Russian outlets have also circulated a variety of fake stories about the downing of the Malaysian airliner MH 17 by pro-Russian rebels, including one claiming it was shot down by Ukrainian forces who thought that Putin was on the plane.

Such propaganda casts the European Union and NATO as aggressors and is often picked up by groups on both the far left and right. By fomenting confusion about the Euromaidan uprising and the alleged fascism of the protesters, it helped prepare the way for the Russia invasion of Ukraine and was a factor in the recent referendum in the Netherlands when Dutch voters disapproved the association agreement between the Ukraine and the EU.

NED is also a target. For example, a fraudulent letter has been circulating online over the last year purporting to show a USAID official asking that NED "revise plans" to use NGOs in Russia, Ukraine, Belarus, and Kazakhstan to recruit people for ISIS, warning of a possible Congressional investigation and media controversy. The letter, undoubtedly the work of Russian trolls, has been picked up by a number of Russian online platforms.

A third soft power front involves an effort to counter international democratic and human rights norms in key rules-based institutions such as the Council of Europe and the Organization for Security and Cooperation in Europe (OSCE), as well as bodies concerned with the governance of the Internet. The goal is to replace established norms contained in the Universal Declaration of Human Rights and other international covenants with alternative norms based on unrestricted state sovereignty and justifying harsh measures against political and ethnic dissidents, who are often called terrorists.

The autocrats have created their own international organizations to advance authoritarian norms globally. Organizations such as the Shanghai Cooperation Organization (which Turkey's President Erdogan recently said that he prefers to the European Union), the Gulf Cooperation Council, and the Eurasian Economic Union work to institutionalize principles that prioritize state sovereignty over human rights concerns. They reinforce domestic repression by helping dictators share techniques of political control and watch lists of dissidents, and they promote state cooperation in the repatriation of dissidents and the cross-border abduction of individuals targeted by security agencies. Just last month dozens of Taiwanese citizens working in Kenya and Malaysia were deported to China, and there have also been cross-border abductions by Chinese authorities of Chinese dissidents in Thailand and booksellers in Hong Kong who sold books critical of China.

Autocratic regimes are also trying to undermine global election norms by stacking international monitoring delegations with what are quaintly called "zombie" monitors who sign off on fraudulent elections. For example, such pseudo-monitors were used to legitimize deeply flawed election processes in Zimbabwe, Azerbaijan, and Venezuela in 2013.

Another arena of soft power competition is cyberspace. Popular sentiment has long held that authoritarian regimes were technologically challenged dinosaurs that could not keep up with online activity and would inevitably be weeded out by the information age. But these regimes are proving much more adaptable than expected. According to a recent statement of the World Movement for Democracy, a global civil society network, authoritarian regimes have prioritized control of cyberspace, developed methods to exert that control, and martialed the resources needed to back their initiatives. National level Internet controls are now deeply entrenched, and authoritarian states are becoming more assertive internationally and regionally, promoting cyber security policies that emphasize concepts of state security at the expense of human rights. They have access to the most sophisticated tools to conduct digital attacks and espionage, to exert digital control over their own populations, and to combat dissent originating beyond their borders.

In sum, the authoritarians are no longer content just to contain democracy. They're now trying to roll it back, and the West has been caught off-guard. This is not the first time that democracy has been put on the defensive and that its prospects have appeared to be bleak. In 1976, on the occasion of the 200th anniversary of the American Declaration of Independence, Daniel Patrick Moynihan wrote in a special bicentennial edition of *The Public Interest* that "Democracy is where the world was, not where the world is going." He said that in the aftermath of the US defeat in Vietnam, the suspension of democracy in India (he had just been the US ambassador there), the fall of many democracies in Latin America, and the rise of "third-world nationalism" and anti-Americanism in the Non-Aligned Movement and other international fora.

Yet as we now know, this bleak moment coincided with what Samuel Huntington was later to identify as the start of the Third Wave of Democratization, which he said in his book by that name was triggered by the fall of the military dictatorship in Portugal on April 25, 1974. The Carnation Revolution, as it was called, was soon followed by Franco's death and the transition in Spain, the spread of democracy across Latin America, the People's Power Revolution in the Philippines, and the great revolutions of 1989 in Central Europe that signaled the end of the Cold War. This was the historic "third wave," which was the greatest expansion of democracy in world history.

Is such a counter-intuitive reversal of negative trends possible today? Obviously this is something we can't know. The current crisis of democracy may be more serious than the setbacks that occurred in the 1970s because US leadership and influence have declined more dramatically. Still, there are a number of reasons not to despair and perhaps even to be cautiously hopeful.

The first is that while the Freedom House annual survey, as mentioned earlier, charts a decline in freedom in many countries, it does not show a decline in the number of electoral democracies in the world, which has held roughly steady at 125, the post- third wave peak level. This is one of the reasons that political scientists like Larry Diamond speak of a "democracy recession" today and not a democracy depression or a "third reverse wave."

Second, there have been a number of surprising advances for democracy. These include the successful presidential election in Nigeria last year, which surprised many people who feared that a stolen election, which they expected, would trigger a deadly civil war. Another key election was the upset victory in Argentina last November of the liberal reformer Mauricio Macri, which *The New York Times* called "a stunner that is likely to set in motion a transformational era at home and in the region." The defeat the following month in Venezuela of the Chavista party in parliamentary elections was also a major setback for illiberal populism in Latin America.

In addition, the National League for Democracy's victory in Burma's elections last November, led by Nobel Laureate Aung San Suu Kyi, was a major step forward. Likewise, the constitutional agreement and democratic election in Tunisia, a process led by the National Dialogue Quartet composed of four civil society organizations that won the Nobel Peace Prize for their efforts, was also a remarkable achievement. Tunisia is now the first democracy in the Arab Middle East. Other positive developments included the surprising defeat in Sri Lanka in 2015 of the extreme Buddhist Nationalists in both presidential and parliamentary elections, and the successful elections in some smaller African countries like Burkina Faso and Cote D'Ivoire.

A third reason for cautious optimism is that the world's resurgent autocrats do not sit securely on their thrones. Their repeated warnings about the danger of foreign-instigated "colored revolutions" is actually an implicit admission that what they fear most is the test of a real election that they might lose, knowing that the trigger for a colored revolution would be an attempt to reverse an unacceptable result. Putin's regime in Russia recently adopted a slate of new draconian laws targeting the upcoming parliamentary elections in September. These laws impose harsher restrictions on monitors, and potentially popular opposition candidates like Alexei Navalny will be prohibited from running. In addition, Putin's formation of a new praetorian guard of 400,000 military personnel under the command of his former personal body guard Viktor Zolotov, a move directed at heading off possible mass protests, is a further sign of regime insecurity. Vladimir Kara-Murza, a political dissident who continues to be active despite an attempt on his life last May, recently asked: "Does this really look like the behavior of a government that has, as it claims, '89 percent' popular support?"

Chinese President Xi also appears insecure in his power. He has greatly tightened political controls, making China more repressive today that at any time since the death of Mao. Yesterday marked the 50th anniversary of the start of the Cultural Revolution in China, a period that is remembered by many as a time of chaos, mass violence (over one million people were killed and tens of millions were tortured and humiliated), and ideological madness. It has been called a "spiritual holocaust." Yet Xi has promoted a cult of Mao and campaigned against "historical nihilism," which is how he terms a critical assessment of Mao's rule, for fear that public discussion of the Mao-led catastrophe might damage the legitimacy of the Communist Party. Xi has been the target of an open letter calling upon him to resign and a sharp remonstrance appearing on the website of the party's own enforcement arm warning that his cult of personality has gone too far. Andy Nathan, who in the past has said that China's party dictatorship has resilience, now writes that Xi's regime "behaves as if it faces an existential threat."

The Castro regime in Cuba also has reason to worry. In the past it has based its legitimacy on standing up to the United States and "imperialism." These ideological props no longer work after the normalization of relations with the United States, and the developments in Argentina and Venezuela make the Cuban dictatorship look increasingly anachronistic. The Castro regime has also increased repression—a sign that it, too, feels vulnerable and insecure. According to opposition leader Manuel Cuesta Morua, 100,000 Cubans have left the Communist Party since 2012.

A fourth reason for cautious optimism is that the world's poorest people have made unprecedented economic, health, and education advances during the last quarter of a century, a phenomenon documented by the Georgetown University development scholar Steven Radelet in his new book *The Great Surge: The Ascent of the Developing World*. According to Radelet, one billion people have been lifted out of poverty since the early 1990s, reducing by half the number of extremely poor people in the world. The child mortality rate has also shrunk drastically, from 10 percent in 1990 to less than 5 percent today (it was 22 percent in 1960). Life expectancy has increased significantly, average incomes have almost doubled, and there have been enormous gains in education, especially for girls, 80 percent of whom now complete primary schools compared to only one-half in 1980. Radelet gives much of the credit for these gains to the expansion of democracy and the rule of law. These factors, in my view, also help account for the sustainability of those gains as measured by Freedom House and for the electoral breakthroughs, since people are much more likely to insist upon respect for their rights as citizens as social, educational, and economic standards rise.

The last reason for hope that I want to point to is the energy and resilience of civil society, not just in fragile new democracies and semi-open autocracies but also in backsliding and increasingly repressive authoritarian countries as well. In Africa they include bloggers in Ethiopia, youth activists and trade unionists in Zimbabwe, investigative journalists in Angola, and human rights defenders and peace activists in Burundi and the Congo, where leaders are dangerously trying to steal or block elections. In Russia, where democratic leaders like Boris Nemtsov have been murdered, activists continue to work fearlessly to expose elite corruption, defend human rights, and offer independent news and information to counter the regime's steady drumbeat of nationalist propaganda. In China, despite the harsh political crackdown, a

Freedom House study reports that more people are joining rights-defense activities, information is spreading despite censorship, the fear of repression is waning, and the disillusionment with party corruption is growing. These examples are just the tip of a massive iceberg of civic activism that exists in all regions of the world and that may at this very moment be preparing the way for new democratic breakthroughs in the future.

We cannot know if a new democratic wave will occur in the foreseeable future. But there are three fundamental things that need to be done to renew democratic progress and momentum. The first is to acknowledge—and try to reverse—the authoritarian resurgence. Congress has awarded NED special funding to develop and implement a strategic plan to address some of the negative trends noted previously, and the Endowment is beginning to carry out that plan, even as the plan continues to be refined as conditions warrant. There is an important role in this effort for private foundations and organizations, both in the US and abroad, and the NED looks forward to working with others and deepening collaboration.

The US government—both the Administration and Congress—must also do more to integrate political support for civil society and democratic freedoms into its regular bi-lateral and multilateral diplomacy, to strenuously defend democratic norms in international and regional rules-based bodies, and to strengthen US capacity in the area of information and international broadcasting. It was a regrettable error to abolish the United States Information Agency (USIA) 15 years ago, but some of the damage can be repaired if Congress passes legislation that is now before it to reform and strengthen US public diplomacy as well as the surrogate radios like RFE/RL that provide alternative news to populations targeted by authoritarian media operations.

The second priority is to restore US leadership in the defense of the liberal world order that is essential for democratic progress, economic growth, and political stability in the world. Such leadership will require a new vision of political and economic

Net Neutrality Is Essential to Democracy

Net neutrality is, simply put, the fundamental principle that all Internet traffic should be treated equally. There are very few level playing fields in American life, but in a nation plagued by inequality, the Internet has remained open, free and fair—a powerful equalizing force that has allowed good ideas to flourish whether they came from a corporate board room or a college dorm room. This equality of opportunity is at the core of net neutrality. And it is under relentless attack by major telecommunications companies seeking yet another advantage to tighten their grip on the market.

Former FCC commissioner Michael Copps has argued that net neutrality is a civil rights issue. "Increasingly, people understand that the Internet is where we go to find jobs, pursue our education, care for our health, manage our finances, conserve energy, interact socially and—importantly—conduct our civic dialogue," writes Copps. "All of which is to say that the Internet is central to our lives and our future. Anyone not having these opportunities is going to be consigned to second-class citizenship." Likewise, Harvard law professor Susan Crawford has called for a "public option" for the Internet, citing the digital divide between socioeconomic classes and noting that the United States lags behind much of the world in high-speed Internet access.

"Net neutrality essential to our democracy," Katrina vanden Heuvel, The Washington Post, December 2, 2014.

cooperation in a globalized world. But that will not be enough. It will also require a new international realism based on the recognition that diplomacy will be ineffective if it is not backed up by power and credible military deterrence. The new realism should also recognize that while engagement with dictatorial regimes is necessary, the US should never conflate a regime that rules without popular consent with the people of a country, or fall into the mirror-image trap of thinking that dictators act according to the same moral and strategic calculus as democratically-elected leaders. Nor should US leaders assume that engagement by itself will produce liberal change if it is not accompanied by significant and sustained human rights pressure and conditionality. No one today proposes that the United States should remake the world in its own image. But that doesn't mean that the US shouldn't support people who share our values and need our help.

Finally, it has become increasingly clear that the US must rebalance the need to promote global trade with the need to protect American manufacturing jobs, particularly against imports from non-democratic and low-wage countries. Bill Galston rightly pointed out recently in *The Wall Street Journal* that we need to make more "aggressive use of anti-dumping provisions in existing trade provisions."

The third priority is to restore our country's sense of purpose in the world and to reaffirm America's founding values that have done so much to inspire and influence the growth of democracy in the world. When Abraham Lincoln stopped at Independence Hall in Philadelphia on his inaugural journey to Washington in February 1861, he remarked that he had "never had a feeling politically that did not spring from the sentiments embodied in the Declaration of Independence," the sentiments involving the equality and unalienable rights of all human beings. He said that he had often inquired of himself "what great principle or idea it was that kept this Confederacy so long together," and he concluded that it was "that sentiment in the Declaration of Independence which gave liberty, not alone to the people of this country, but, I hope, for the world, for all future time."

That is the source of America's greatness, and that greatness will not be restored just by loudly proclaiming that America needs to be great again, especially when that call is accompanied by a rejection of the idea that democratic values are universal and that US ideals and interests are served by trying to advance them beyond the established democracies of the West.

As a matter of fact, with the democratic West absorbed as it is today in its own problems, the effort to advance democracy is being led not by the West but by the global democracy movement—the people and organizations on the ground in one country after another in the global south and post-communist world who are fighting to defend their rights and human dignity. It is there—more than in the West today—that one hears the language of democratic solidarity and universal human rights. It is my hope that by linking young Americans and Europeans with young activists and others fighting for fundamental rights and freedoms in the non-Western countries of the world, this might spark a revival of democratic commitment in the Western countries where democracy, after many trials, first took root.

It is ironic that the United States and other Western countries should need democratic inspiration from the very people they should be helping. But that will encourage humility, a virtue that will be needed in abundance as we try to respond effectively to the immense challenges that lie ahead in a dangerous and complex world.

Periodical and Internet Sources Bibliography

The following articles have been selected to supplement the diverse views presented in this chapter.

Hannah Aitchison, "How Can Schools Engage Young People in Democracy?" *Guardian*, May 17, 2017. https://www.theguardian.com/teacher-network/2017/may/17/how-can-schools-engage-young-people-in-democracy.

Arthur Camins, "Why Science Education Is Essential for Democracy," *HuffPost* blog, October 31, 2016. http://www.huffingtonpost.com/arthur-camins/why-science-education-is-_b_12692726.html.

Economist, "What's Gone Wrong with Democracy? Democracy Was the Most Successful Political Idea of the 20th Century. Why Has It Run Into Trouble, and What Can Be Done to Revive It?" http://www.economist.com/news/essays/21596796-democracy-was-most-successful-political-idea-20th-century-why-has-it-run-trouble-and-what-can-be-do.

Betty Sue Flowers, "Western Democracy Needs a New Narrative," *Open Democracy*, April 27, 2017. https://www.opendemocracy.net/betty-sue-flowers/western-democracy-needs-new-narrative.

Yascha Mounk and Roberto Stefan Foa, "Yes, People Really Are Turning Away from Democracy," *Washington Post*, December 8, 2016. https://www.washingtonpost.com/news/wonk/wp/2016/12/08/yes-millennials-really-are-surprisingly-approving-of-dictators/?utm_term=.4fff9101ddd4.

Bill Moyers, "We the Plutocrats vs. We the People," *Salon*, September 12, 2016. http://www.salon.com/2016/09/12/we-the-plutocrats-vs-we-the-people-how-to-save-democracy-in-america_partner.

Adele Peters, "Can Technology Save Democracy?" *Fast Company*, March 13, 2017. https://www.fastcompany.com/3068382/can-technology-save-democracy.

James Stavridis, "Former Supreme Allied Commander: Why NATO Is a Necessity," *Time*, April 4, 2016. http://time.com/4281029/nato-is-a-necessity.

For Further Discussion

Chapter 1

1. Do you agree that *Citizens United* has damaged democracy? Why or why not?
2. Do you think the US Constitution was designed to protect property rights more than the rights of citizens to the basic necessities of life, and a voice in government? Does this interpretation of the Constitution have any validity today?
3. Do you think that average citizens have the tools to make well-informed decisions about important issues? Explain how this could weaken democracy.

Chapter 2

1. Do you agree that the issue of property rights leads to unethical or corrupt governments? Why or why not?
2. What is the role of parties in a democracy? Do you think a two-party system is best, or would more political parties make for a more vibrant democracy? Explain.
3. What do you think might be done to shore up democracy in the West?

Chapter 3

1. Why do you think the Founding Fathers wanted to put limits on democracy? Do those reason still apply today?
2. What sorts of activities seem to you to be essential to democratic participation? Why do you think many of these actions are local rather than national?
3. Do you see any advantages to a system in which states with smaller populations get a disproportionate say in government? If you think that the system is fundamentally undemocratic and unfair, can you think of a way that it

might be changed to give more equal representation to individual citizens?

Chapter 4

1. Do you agree that an educated populace is essential for a functioning democracy? Why or why not?
2. What sorts of skills do you think are essential for good citizenship? Where would one acquire those skills?
3. Do you think that the rise of so-called "fake news" and distorted reporting has damaged democracy in the West? Explain.

Organizations to Contact

The editors have compiled the following list of organizations concerned with the issues debated in this book. The descriptions are derived from materials provided by the organizations. All have publications or information available for interested readers. The list was compiled on the date of publication of the present volume; the information provided here may change. Be aware that many organizations take several weeks or longer to respond to inquiries, so allow as much time as possible.

American Civil Liberties Union (ACLU)
125 Broad Street, 18th Floor, New York, NY 10001
(212) 549-2500
website: www.aclu.org

The ACLU is an organization that works to defend and protect the individual rights and liberties that are guaranteed by the Constitution of the United States.

American Library Association Office for Intellectual Freedom
50 East Huron Street
Chicago, IL 60611
(312) 280-4226
email: oif@ala.org
website: www.ala.org

This arm of the ALA is responsible for implementing the organization's policies on intellectual freedom. Sponsors education, training, and public awareness programs.

Brennan Center for Justice
120 Broadway
Suite 1750
New York, NY 10271
(646) 292-8310
email: brennancenter@nyu.edu
website: www.brennancenter.org

A nonpartisan law and policy institute that works to hold the United States to its promises of democracy and equal justice for all, including efforts to protect voting rights.

Canadian Civil Liberties Association
90 Eglinton Ave E.
Toronto, ON M4P 2Y3
(416) 363-0321
email: mail@ccla.org
website: www.ccla.org

The Canadian Civil Liberties Association is an organization fighting for the civil liberties, human rights, and democratic freedoms of people all across Canada.

Generation Citizen
175 Varick Street, 5th Floor
New York, NY, 10014
(And other locations)
website: www.generationcitizen.org

Generation Citizen is an organization dedicated to empowering young people to become engaged and effective citizens, by providing them with the knowledge and skills to participate in democracy.

International Republican Institute
1225 I Street, NW, Suite 800
Washington, DC. 20005
(202) 408-9450
email: info@iri.org
website: www.iri.org

International Republican Institute is a non-profit organization working to support freedom and democracy worldwide. Has women and youth leadership programs.

National Democratic Institute
455 Massachusetts Ave, NW, 8th Floor
Washington, DC 20001-2621
(202)728-5500
website: www.ndi.org

A nonprofit, nonpartisan organization that works to strengthen civic organizations, safeguard elections, and promote citizen participation, openness, and accountability in government.

National Endowment for Democracy (NED)
1025 F Street NW, Suite 800
Washington, D.C. 20004
(202) 378-9700
email: info@NED.org
website: www.ned.org

NED is a private, nonprofit organization dedicated to the growth and strengthening of democratic institutions around the world.

Rock the Vote
1875 Connecticut Ave, NW 10th Floor
Washington, DC 20009
(202) 719-9649
website: www.rockthevote.com

Rock the Vote is a nonprofit organization dedicated to building the political power of young people.

Running Start
1310 L Street NW
Washington, DC 20005
(202) 223-3895
email: info@runningstartonline.org
website: http://runningstartonline.org

Running Start is an organization that educates young women about politics and gives them the skills they need to be leaders.

Bibliography of Books

Christopher H. Achen and Larry M. Bartels, *Democracy for Realists: Why Elections Do Not Produce Responsive Government*. Princeton, NJ: Princeton University Press, 2016.

Bruce Bartlett, *Truth Matters: A Citizen's Guide to Separating Fact from Lies and Stopping Fake News in Its Tracks*. Emeryville, CA: Ten Speed Press, 2017.

Jason Brennan, *Against Democracy*. Princeton, NJ: Princeton University Press, 2016.

Tim Lacy, *The Dream of a Democratic Culture: Mortimer Adler and the Great Books Idea*. New York, NY: Palgrave Macmillan, 2013.

Sinclair Lewis, *It Can't Happen Here* (novel). New York, NY: Signet (reprint education), 2014.

Mark Lilla, *The Shipwrecked Mind: On Political Reaction*. New York, NY: New York Review Books, 2016.

Peter Mair, *Ruling the Void: The Hollowing of Western Democracy*. London, UK: Verso, 2013.

Cas Mudde and Cristobal Rovira Kaltwasser, *Populism: A Very Short Introduction*. Oxford, UK: Oxford University Press, 2017.

Condoleezza Rice, *Democracy: Stories from the Long Road to Freedom*. New York, NY: Twelve, 2017.

Michael T. Rogers, ed. *Civic Education in the Twenty-first Century: A Multidimensional Inquiry*. Lanham, MD: Lexington Books, 2015.

Jason Stanley, *How Propaganda Works*. Princeton, NJ: Princeton University Press, 2016.

Index

E

F

G

H

I

J

K

L

M

N

O

P

R

S

T

U

V

W